INBOUND

PR

INBOUND

PR

The PR Agency's Manual
to Transforming Your Business
with **Inbound**

ILIYANA STAREVA

WILEY

For general information about our other products and services, please contact our Customer
Care Department within the United States at (800) 762-2974, outside the United States at
(317) 572-3993 or fax (317) 572-4002.

Wiley publishes in a variety of print and electronic formats and by print-on-demand.
Some material included with standard print versions of this book may not be included in
e-books or in print-on-demand. If this book refers to media such as a CD or DVD that is
not included in the version you purchased, you may download this material
at http://booksupport.wiley.com. For more information about Wiley products,
visit www.wiley.com.

Library of Congress Cataloging-in-Publication Data

Names: Stareva, Iliyana, author.
Title: Inbound PR : the PR agency's manual to transforming your business with
  inbound / Iliyana Stareva.
Description: Hoboken : Wiley, 2018. | Includes bibliographical references and index. |
Identifiers: LCCN 2017039797 (print) | LCCN 2017041284 (ebook) |
  ISBN 9781119462279 (pdf) | ISBN 9781119462255 (epub) |
  ISBN 9781119462217 (hardback)
Subjects: LCSH: Marketing. | Selling. | Customer relations. | Public relations. |
  BISAC: BUSINESS & ECONOMICS / Public Relations. | BUSINESS & ECONOMICS /
  Marketing / General. | BUSINESS & ECONOMICS / Sales & Selling.
Classification: LCC HF5415 (ebook) | LCC HF5415 .S7473 2017 (print) | DDC
  658.8–dc23
LC record available at https://lccn.loc.gov/2017039797

Printed in the United States of America

10 9 8 7 6 5 4 3 2 1

Contents

The New World of Inbound PR:
A Foreword

Respond to this statement with a "yes" or "no": *The job of a public relations agency is to get ink and airtime from the media.*

For decades, the correct response was yes, because we didn't have any choice.

Back in the day, the only way to easily communicate with your public was to use mainstream media and analysts as your mouthpieces. So the public relations department and the agencies they employed spent a great deal of effort convincing editors, reporters, and analysts that your company was one worth writing about. Prior to gaining the ability to self-publish content, there wasn't an efficient way for organizations to communicate directly to the public, so we were stuck with using the media as our mouthpiece.

That's exactly what I did for nearly a decade. As the vice president of marketing for several different technology companies, I had to work with agencies to pitch our story to the media. Occasionally, we got mentioned in a newspaper or magazine article or got airtime on television or radio. But it was really hard work and damned expensive.

Today, the correct response to my statement is an emphatic *no!*

In our new world of real-time engagement, there are so many other ways to communicate with your publics. There has been an explosion of channels and content that organizations can use to reach their audience directly with valuable online content: videos; e-books; white papers; photos; infographics; social networks like Facebook, LinkedIn, and Snapchat; and more. Now we reach buyers directly, and they are eager to share our content.

However, many PR professionals still operate as if their only conduit is mainstream media. Most agencies still only use the traditional press release and pitch strategy.

If your organization operates in this outdated way, you've got to change the way you do business. Fortunately, you are reading the right book to help guide you with that transition.

Iliyana Stareva comes from the PR trenches. She worked in PR agencies in several countries and personally implemented many of the ideas you will read in these pages. This is no academic tome; instead, it offers practical and proven advice for reaching customers directly.

Iliyana is currently Global Partner Program Manager at HubSpot, an inbound marketing and sales software company. I've seen Iliyana in action because I serve on the advisory board of HubSpot. I frequently encounter her smart blog posts and social networking posts. In her work at HubSpot, she's met with the leaders of several hundred agencies, and she draws from those interactions to make this book perfectly positioned to help agencies make the transition.

In this new world, which Iliyana calls inbound PR, smart public relations pros realize they have a tremendous opportunity to communicate directly with their publics. They are transforming themselves and their agencies into content creators. And they are helping their clients grow their businesses.

I use these ideas myself and they work!

—David Meerman Scott
Marketing and public relations strategist, entrepreneur, and
best-selling author of 10 books, including *The New Rules of
Marketing & PR* and *Newsjacking*
www.WebInkNow.com
@dmscott

Modernizing Public Relations and Marketing: A Foreword

The role of the old is to inspire the young. But often the young inspire the old.

This book is about an innovative application of modern public relations. But it's also a young woman's story about innovation, motivation and hard work.

I first met Iliyana Stareva in Dublin in October 2015. I sought her out on a visit to the city after reading her blog, and seeing her work at HubSpot on the inbound PR model. I'm a long-time fan of Iliyana's blog. She uses it as a means of thinking out loud, and sharing ideas. She's earned a reputation as a forward thinking practitioner in marketing and public relations. Iliyana has used her blog to help develop her thinking. She's generous in publishing her ideas, and as a result has built a community that supports her work through conversation and sharing. It's a highly effective form of learning that requires both bravery and humility, characteristics which Iliyana possesses in abundance.

I first learned about inbound PR from Iliyana's blog. It's a means of identifying and understanding an audience or public and using content to start a conversation. It's made possible thanks to a growing industry of data, media and tools, to help understand behavior on the internet and social web. Inbound PR seeks to build a relationship based on an organization meeting a need rather than creating a need. It lies at the heart of the difference between public relations and marketing. It's a subtle but important point of difference. The internet is full of spam and unwanted marketing content. Inbound PR enables an individual or organization to build relationships and trust, and influence behavior. It's a highly effective form of lead generation in business-to-business or professional services, although its application is by no means limited to this sphere.

The inbound PR model has been stress tested in Iliyana's day job at HubSpot where she helps agencies around the world get to grips with the tools they need to execute content marketing campaigns. She's a regular speaker at HubSpot events, and has joined the international speaker circuit in the footsteps of the likes of Seth Godin, David Meerman-Scott and Brian Solis to share her ideas. She has written extensively for a variety of industry publications, including #FuturePRoof and Spin Sucks.

In Dublin, we talked about how Iliyana could develop her thinking and writing on inbound PR into a book. I followed up after our meeting with a list of potential publishers. It's a testament to Iliyana's drive and motivation that 18 months later she sent me a proof of *Inbound PR*, and the news that she'd landed a publishing deal with Wiley. *Inbound PR* codifies the model that Iliyana devised, and describes its application in practice. The book is written very much in the style of her blog. It's clear, concise and highly informative. You'll have no problem in applying her teaching in your work.

I couldn't be more proud of Iliyana for what she's achieved.

—Stephen Waddington
Partner and Chief Engagement Officer, Ketchum
Visiting Professor, Newcastle University

Introduction

I come from a public relations (PR) background. I spent three years working in PR agencies across Germany and the United Kingdom. I loved it but I saw the flaws, too, and so I moved away from the industry, transitioning into something more modern: inbound marketing and agency business consulting.

It turns out I was wrong. For two and a half years, I consulted over 200 agencies in my role as a Channel Consultant at HubSpot—the inbound marketing and sales software as a service pioneer—and I realized that I'm never getting away from PR. I still researched it and I still wrote about it. I still saw the flaws and I still wanted to fix them.

Thankfully, I saw a way. A way that can transform the public relations industry. A way that can transform the PR agency model.

It started with a simple realization: the way we make decisions has fundamentally changed, regardless of whether that concerns our personal or our professional lives. We've become a lot more sophisticated and we feel empowered to go online, do our research, talk to friends, read recommendations, tweet at companies with questions, and demand answers to our problems through the content that we find. We don't want to be marketed at; we want the freedom to choose, based on our own online experiences.

Content is the name of the buying game today.

And who's better suited to create fascinating content and use it to engage with the public than PR practitioners?

Marketers, advisers, and digital professionals struggle with content creation, but they are good at numbers, data, and measurement—something PR professionals are still at odds with.

Enter inbound PR, where content meets measurement and helps PR people show the real return on investment (ROI) of their efforts in the new digital era.

So, there are two main reasons why inbound is the perfect fit for PR:

1. PR people excel at content creation.
2. PR people suck at measurement.

PR professionals are the best content creators. They are natural storytellers—this is how it has been since the first press release. Writing and communication skills have been at the forefront of PR practitioners' skillsets, but not so much for marketing, advertising, or digital agency professionals.

On the other hand, PR people are very bad at measurement. Showing the tangible results of their efforts in a way that makes sense to the bottom line has been the single biggest challenge for PR since its very beginning.

Especially in the digital era, you can't be using outputs or metrics such as advertising value equivalents (AVEs) or impressions; you must be able to measure outcomes and show the real impact on the business that is often defined by an increase in sales.

Inbound makes measurement possible; however, it doesn't work without content.

By now, you as a PR agency owner who is struggling to take your agency to the next level are hopefully hooked, so let me ask you some questions:

1. Do you blog?
2. Do you use social media?
3. Do you have a landing page on your website?
4. How much time do you invest in doing PR for your own agency or communications team?

Let me take a guess the answers:

1. Hmm, when we have time.
2. Yes, but mainly just to curate or share our own stuff.
3. No, no time for that and what's the point.
4. We just don't have time because we are too busy with client work.

Now you might be thinking, "Why do I even need any of that? We have our clients, our team is busy, we can't invest time and money into something that won't bring us much results."

This is the number one challenge for agencies—we don't have time for our own PR and marketing.

I know agency life, and believe me, I sympathize with the workload, and I know how demanding clients can be. But for me, not having time is an excuse. Think of it this way: you really want to lose weight, so you need to fix up your diet and work out five times per week. However, you are super busy at work and at home, so you know that to achieve your goal you need to develop some new routines and adjust your daily lifestyle. That includes finding or better yet making the time for working out and preparing healthy food and snacks. There are two possible scenarios here: you find excuses and don't make the time and so you don't see any results, but you are still frustrated and angry as nothing is happening; or you've made a conscious choice to change and make the time (for example, through calendar planning) and you are seeing some fantastic progress.

As a PR agency owner or CEO, which one will you choose: being stuck in the state where you've always been, or will you embrace change?

I hope it's the latter because doing your own PR with your own content and promoting it on your own channels is the best thing you could ever do for your team or agency. Why? Because inbound PR can help you build brand awareness, generate leads (customer or media), nurture them, close them as customers or publishers, and then delight them to retain them with even better services, stories, and strong relationships. Most importantly, you'll be able to track the ROI of all those activities. And once you can do this for your agency, then you'll be able to develop the inbound PR services and the internal capabilities to deliver them for clients. That's how you'll grow your PR business in the twenty-first century.

This book is about you. Just as inbound is.

In a typical inbound fashion, each chapter will educate you on particular topics that all build upon each other so that you can move from learning to doing.

In Chapter 1, we'll look at the definitions of public relations and inbound marketing, what the two disciplines do and where the similarities are. We'll also see what binds them. We'll lay a foundation of common knowledge.

Chapter 2 is dedicated to PR's biggest challenge—measurement—and covers the current status quo, the history of communications measurement, how measurement works with inbound, where the opportunity for PR lies, and what the future of PR measurement looks like.

In Chapter 3, I'll take you on the journey of how I came up with the inbound PR concept, its definitions and benefits, and why you as a PR agency (or any communications agency) should adopt it.

Once we have this theory covered, I'll introduce you to the inbound PR methodology in Chapter 4 and offer you a lot of practical advice and tips on how to run inbound PR campaigns, how to create remarkable content, and how to tell inbound stories. This chapter has a strong focus on how to work with journalists, influencers, and media people in an inbound way as well as how to create inbound PR newsrooms.

Chapter 5 will delve into the importance and development of a strong positioning strategy for your agency that will then ultimately help you generate new business, nurture leads, and close the leads in your sales funnel.

Finally, in Chapter 6, we'll cover how to define and package inbound PR services into 12-month client retainers and how to develop the knowledge, capabilities, and skills your people need to be able to deliver inbound PR and to drive client results.

PR is ripe for transformation. Are you ready to embark on the inbound PR journey?

About the Author

Iliyana Stareva lives and breathes inbound marketing and PR for agencies. Iliyana spent three years in the PR industry throughout Germany and the United Kingdom, establishing the presence of some of the largest fast-moving consumer goods brands in the world in those markets. She was then recruited by HubSpot—the leading marketing and sales software as a service pioneer—to become one of its first agency business consultants in Dublin, Ireland, where she helped dozens of marketing, content, PR, and web agencies double or triple their revenues. It was during that time that Iliyana developed the inbound PR concept.

Earning rapid promotions at HubSpot, Iliyana is now Global Partner Program Manager, focused on aligning HubSpot's expanding global teams and helping agency partners grow within the program.

Iliyana is also the author of *Social Media and the Rebirth of PR: The Emergence of Social Media as a Change Driver for PR* (2013) and *Social Media—Key for Sustainability Communications* (2013).

Iliyana spends her free time dancing salsa or writing about inbound PR, inbound marketing, and agency business on her blog at www.iliyanastareva.com.

Acknowledgments

Huge thanks to my family for the support provided when I was writing this, especially to my mom, Teodora Stareva, for always encouraging me and being there for me.

Special thanks to Stephen Waddington for getting the idea in my head to write a book about inbound PR.

Chapter 1

Getting the Basics

PR and Inbound

What Is Public Relations?

Whenever we try to explain a term, we tend to start with the textbook definitions that students learn when they go to university.

Public relations (PR) certainly is a mystery to many people, including some working in the industry or studying it.

The Public Relations Society of America which is the leading PR organization in the world, defines public relations as "the strategic communication process that builds mutually beneficial relationships between an organization and its publics" (PRSA, 2017).

The Chartered Institute of Public Relations the other leading PR body based in the United Kingdom—argues that "public relations is the discipline which looks after reputation, with the aim of earning understanding and support and influencing opinion and behavior. It is the planned and sustained effort to establish and maintain goodwill and mutual understanding between an organization and its publics" (CIPR, 2017).

Now admittedly, these two definitions are a bit hard to grasp as they entail a number of buzzwords such as "mutually beneficial," "influencing," "goodwill," and so on.

If you read Guy Kawasaki's book *The Macintosh Way* (1989, 123), you'll see a quote by Jean-Louis Gassee—a former Apple executive—explaining that advertising is saying that you're good, whereas PR is getting someone else to say that you're good.

This definition is easier to grasp, right?

It doesn't tell us exactly what PR people do, but at least it strengthens the point that PR is concerned with organizational reputation and building meaningful and positive relationships between various audiences.

For most of its existence, dating back to the beginning of the twentieth century, PR has mainly dealt with media relations, events, reputation, crisis management, and investor relations. In fact, for a very long time public relations and media relations (or publicity) have been considered synonymous, where PR people write press releases and send them to journalists who then use those press releases to write stories for their publications and media outlets—newspapers, magazines, TV, radio, and so on.

Many are under that same assumption today, which is what has been driving PR's own reputation.

But with the emergence of digital technology and its mass adoption, this understanding is outdated, because PR is not just media relations—and it *shouldn't* be just media relations.

Heavily relying on the media and pitching them press releases has been the traditional view of PR, but with the growth of digital media, the need for an intermediary—the media—to spread the information has diminished. PR can now engage directly with customers, prospects, investors, and any stakeholder group using online channels to send key messages through various means such as articles, blog posts, e-books, social media, comments, and video.

Digital is the reason why the arsenal of PR activities has increased enormously. Media relations can simply be one of those activities. More and more PR people are now responsible for generating leads as well as nurturing them to help sales close new business. They do this by making use of content marketing (e-books, whitepapers, reports, videos, podcasts, webinars, blog posts), e-mail marketing, social media, search engine optimization (SEO), blogger relations, influencer relations, online reputation management, crisis communications, and more.

But the problem with the PR industry has always been this: it's been too slow to adapt to changes and jump on the bandwagon of new technological developments. This happened with social media a few years back when the use of social channels was just starting to peak. Many felt that PR should be the owner of social because PR pros are the people who build mutually beneficial relationships with communities—basically what social media is all about. Unfortunately, PR was a bit too slow and so social media agencies arose, advertising agencies won social media awards, and so on. A similar thing happened with SEO as well, but let's not get into that here.

The reality is that PR needs to reinvent itself. PR needs to change the widespread perception that it's just about media relations. It needs to show that it's able to grow, adapt, and adjust for the digital economy and show sustainable results to clients. Because if PR continues to stick with the conventional ways of thinking, it's not going be relevant or important.

And here's where the link between PR and inbound begins: using the inbound marketing methodology to drive tangible and trackable results.

So, what's inbound then?

What Is Inbound?

The way we make decisions and buy things has fundamentally changed. We used to rely on direct sales and direct mail, or on television and magazine advertising and media publications. We couldn't do much research; we didn't need much convincing as the array of choice for products and services wasn't as vast as it is today.

But we are a lot more sophisticated and empowered now. We do our research online, we check recommendations on social, we read and get information, we compare vendors and products, we barely speak to sales reps because we prefer the advice from peers and friends on social media. We do all that on our own, at our preferred time, using our favorite devices, apps, and websites. Essentially, we make decisions based on the content that we find when we need it.

We don't like when something—such as advertisements—interrupts this process, and we tend to skip them. But we like to be engaged, enticed, and drawn into something interesting.

That's what inbound is all about. It's about attracting people with the right content.

In essence, inbound is about getting found. It's about creating remarkable content and sharing it with the world so that people can find it and come to you, instead of you having to find and chase them.

As HubSpot puts it, the inbound methodology is "the best way to turn strangers into customers and promoters of your business." It's more scalable, efficient, and cost-effective than traditional outbound techniques.

The major difference between the old-school outbound approach and the new inbound method is the notion of pushing versus pulling people in. Outbound marketers predominantly used to (and many still do) push their messages with top-down, interruptive communications and activities. Inbound marketers, on the other hand, use multichannel techniques that earn people's attention and trust by engaging with relevant content. By creating and fostering such meaningful, two-way dialogues, often driven by social media, people come to you on their own; you are not chasing them. This is marketing that people love. Why? Because it's seamless, transparent, authentic, engaging, empowering, and value-adding. It's human.

The inbound marketing methodology is based on four key actions that help turn strangers into promoters of the business: attract, convert, close, and delight. Inbound marketing relies on specific channels, tools, and techniques to guide strangers through the different stages of the methodology (see Figure 1.1).

Inbound marketing is more effective than traditional marketing because it uses blogs, e-books, whitepapers, videos, SEO, webinars, and social, whereas traditional outbound marketing relies on cold calling, TV and print ads, direct mail, and

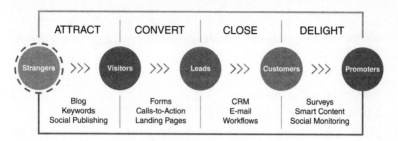

FIGURE 1.1 Inbound Marketing Methodology
Source: © HubSpot.

trade shows, which people nowadays know how to ignore, using things such as caller ID and ad blocking, spam filters, and so on. To give you an example, a 2015 research study from Fractl and Moz on outbound and inbound marketing concluded that consumers are fed up with low-value, high-noise marketing.[1]

The key difference then is that outbound interrupts, inbound attracts. And it attracts with content.

We attract strangers to our website with blogs, social media posts, and SEO; we convert these strangers into leads through higher value content that we gate behind forms on landing pages that require visitors to provide their e-mail addresses (or Facebook and Google log-ins); we then nurture those leads with e-mail (which again provides content) to offer them even more value and turn them into clients. It doesn't end there. We continue to provide relevant content to delight and retain clients, because acquiring new customers can be anywhere from 5 to 25 times more expensive than retaining existing ones.[2]

All of this can be achieved through your website and online channels if you commit to it, develop a content strategy that covers each of those steps, and continuously create that content (on your own) and heavily promote it so that it can spread.

Nowadays, there's rarely a need to be offline with your marketing. In fact, inbound marketing is more than strong enough to bring you customers because for 57 percent of marketers inbound practices provide the highest quality leads to sales.[3]

Content: The Glue between Inbound and PR

There's one thing that has been mentioned again and again in the previous few pages: content.

Both PR and inbound marketing heavily rely on content. Remarkable content is, in fact, the key ingredient of each practice. It's also the glue between the two.

We've said that PR is all about reputation and engaging in meaningful relationships with various publics.

In today's society, driven by digital, that engagement predominantly happens online. The only way to drive it is through content.

Content is something that PR people do better than anyone else in the creative industry—marketers, advertisers, web or digital experts. PR professionals are natural storytellers—writing and creating content for a particular audience is what they do day in and day out; it's what they learn when they go to college. Content that is audience-driven, strategically thought-out, and high-quality engages, entices, and converts visitors on your landing pages and website.

On the other hand, marketers and other digital professionals tend to struggle with content; it's a challenge because their specialty is data or technology rather than content creation. They think with numbers in mind not stories.

During my time as Channel Consultant at HubSpot, I worked with over 200 agencies from various backgrounds and I saw this firsthand. PR and communications professionals have no problem creating regular and consistent content; every other agency professional does.

This was the first realization that I had when inbound PR was materializing in my head.

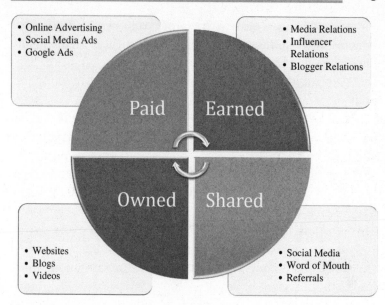

- Online Advertising
- Social Media Ads
- Google Ads

- Media Relations
- Influencer Relations
- Blogger Relations

Paid   Earned

Owned   Shared

- Websites
- Blogs
- Videos

- Social Media
- Word of Mouth
- Referrals

FIGURE 1.2 PESO

But when I actually began working on the concept, the starting point was to look at the four types of media (see Figure 1.2) that we have today: paid, earned, shared, and owned (PESO).

When we think again about PR being considered just media relations or publicity, we can see that this notion hasn't gone away. It falls under earned media; we are still earning coverage in various media outlets that people continue to read, follow, or buy.

Shared media is all about social media and channels that we use daily as they have become extremely important in our personal and professional lives: Facebook, Twitter, LinkedIn, Instagram, and so on.

Paid media is gaining in importance because we live in an information overload era so when we use native and social advertising or sponsored content we ensure that our message truly reaches our intended audience. Today, without paid, your messages are pretty much dead.

And then we have owned media. Owned media has become hugely, hugely important over the last decade with the emergence of blogs and the necessity for businesses to have websites and a social presence with their own content online. That's inbound.

When we look at all of the media types, it's content that's at the center of them. Relevant content designed for a particular audience or a particular media type is at the center of PR and it's at the center of inbound marketing, too.

PR professionals understand audiences, and they know how to take a small bit of news and turn it into an entire story. This is where they excel, and it is what they do every day.

Inbound marketers use content to convert leads to give to sales. Without it, they simply can't follow the inbound marketing methodology.

Inbound PR itself arose through content.

In the spring of 2015, I started experimenting with the concept.

I have a blog that turned six on January 1, 2018. It took me three years to develop an audience that now averages about 10,000 visits per month with a 30- to 40-percent conversion rate on my landing pages.

Blogging is my thought process; it's my way of experimenting and learning. So I started researching and writing about this idea of inbound PR. And people were interested. They were sharing and commenting about how it all makes sense. Therefore, I continued working on this concept.

The moment when it hit me that inbound PR had become a thing was when Sarah Hall—a PR practitioner from the United Kingdom—reached out to me to ask me to contribute a chapter on inbound PR for the first edition of *#FuturePRoof* last autumn. *#FuturePRoof* is a crowdsourced book of essays contributed by more than 30 global PR professionals with the goal to increase awareness of how PR needs to reinvent itself to be viewed as a management discipline.[4]

The moment when it hit me that I really need to write this book was my 2016 talk at INBOUND—the biggest inbound conference in the world with over 19,000 visitors. Speaking in front of 300 people about inbound PR and seeing the positive feedback afterward and the array of questions and people wanting to learn how to do it was the ultimate proof that inbound PR is here to stay.

This is how inbound PR was born: out of the realization that it makes sense to combine PR's biggest strength (content) and alleviate its biggest challenge (measurement) with inbound and to create content to share through blog posts, slideshows, social media, books, and talks around the world to see if it will pull people in. It came about through a lot of research and writing and it ultimately serves the belief that digital is about connecting with people through content. It's content that drives our thoughts and decision-making, but when we flip it into the business world, we also need to figure out its return on investment.

Chapter 2

PR and Measurement

The History of Measurement in Public Relations and Communications

The single biggest challenge that PR pros have been facing since the very birth of the industry has been measurement.

Just google PR measurement and you'll see tons of articles explaining how advertising value equivalents (AVEs) don't work, how we need a new set of tools to measure PR results, how PR hasn't adjusted to the new era of digital and metrics, and so on.

The problems associated with measuring the effectiveness of PR have their roots in a lot of insecurities over the last century within the PR industry itself and a number of failed attempts to find a measurement framework that can be universally accepted and approved not just by PR professionals themselves but also by clients, stakeholders, shareholders, and other interest groups.

If you do a little bit of research into the topic of measurement for communications you'll no doubt find Professor Tom Watson of Bournemouth University in England, who has been researching public relations measurement and evaluation for the past 20 years. He says: "I'd like to say that it's a story of continuous improvement in public relations practice and its measurement and evaluation, but that's not the case. I find that the emphasis on consumer and marketing-led PR since the 1950s has fostered poor practices, although major corporations have moved ahead" (Watson, 2011).

This inability to find one way to measure PR and prove its worth to the bottom line is what has driven the industry's negative perception and reputation. A lot of people have a firm belief that PR cannot be measured and so choose not to invest in it, which, in turn, causes the industry to suffer.

So how did PR get there?

Mainly by relying on metrics and methods that are quantifiable but absolutely irrelevant as they don't relate back to business goals and outcomes but rather to tactical outputs, particularly focused on the results of publicity or typical media relations, as we said earlier.

Let's take a look at some of those irrelevant metrics:

♦ Media impressions: This is the number of visitors a certain publication has. No matter how spectacular your article is, it's not going be read by absolutely every one of those visitors nor could you be certain that those people really are your ideal target audience. This is why impressions as a metric tell you nothing about whether you've reached the right people and the right number of people you need to hit your business goals.

♦ Number of placements or clippings: This is about calculating in how many media outlets you appeared. As with impressions, counting how many mentions your company has received tells you nothing about whether those mentions have brought you customers.

Now you see, these two were used back in the 1930s and 1940s by the U.S. government and, ironically, are still used today, as Professor Watson explains in his research paper, "The Evolution of Evaluation—the Accelerating March Towards the Measurement of Public Relations Effectiveness" (Watson, 2011a, 5–6).

AVEs? Still?

But there's another, even more dangerous metric: advertising value equivalents (AVEs). This method arose with the increasing focus of management on the bottom line as an attempt to find a way to show the dollar value of PR activities.

AVEs involve calculating column inches of published articles or the earned seconds of airtime on TV and radio and multiplying the total of those by the advertising rate of the media where the coverage appeared.

AVEs are still being used today although they are flawed and often misleading. Here are some of the reasons they are not well suited for use today:

- The publicity could be negative so you can't compare it with advertising, which is always positive because you pay big money for it and therefore control the message.
- The articles could mention competitors or speak more positively about other companies than yours, unlike advertising, which is just about your brand because you pay for it.
- The editorials could appear in totally irrelevant media channels where no one from your target audience is. You probably wouldn't do that with advertising as it's expensive and you'd be very careful where you put your money.

But the most significant reason for the ineffectiveness of AVEs is that they measure cost—not value—by calculating the equivalent media space and time for advertising thus making the method flawed. In his PR Metrics Report, Jim Macnamara from the University of Technology Sydney exclaims, "No one in marketing or management would measure the value of advertising simply in terms of its cost—it must be a good campaign because it cost $7 million!" (Macnamara 2015, 34).

What's more, some PR professionals not only compare advertising rates but go beyond that to add multipliers of the respective ad value that are three, four, or five times higher or even more. They do this because editorial and media content is supposed to be more credible and valuable than self-promotional advertising.

But let's not forget that PR today is not just publicity or media relations, so AVEs can't help in the world of digital and social media communications. Would you really compare the advertising rate for a tweet?

THE BARCELONA PRINCIPLES

Luckily, the Barcelona Principles were developed in 2010 urging PR pros to move away from advertising value equivalents and agree upon a new, minimum standard of measurement that actually shows the value of PR for an organization.

The Barcelona Principles comprise seven guidelines to measurement that focus on outcomes and business results rather than media results and outputs.[1]

The first version of the Barcelona Principles was introduced in 2010 as follows:

1. Importance of Goal Setting and Measurement
2. Measuring the Effect on Outcomes Is Preferred to Measuring Outputs
3. The Effect on Business Results Can and Should Be Measured Where Possible
4. Media Measurement Requires Quantity and Quality
5. AVEs Are Not the Value of Public Relations
6. Social Media Can and Should Be Measured
7. Transparency and Replicability Are Paramount to Sound Measurement

In 2015, a revised and updated version was published to serve as a foundation to any communications program or function, not just for PR. Here's how the guidelines were updated:[2]

1. Goal Setting and Measurement Are Fundamental to Communication and Public Relations
2. Measuring Communication Outcomes Is Recommended Versus Only Measuring Outputs

3. The Effect on Organizational Performance Can and Should Be Measured Where Possible

4. Measurement and Evaluation Require Both Qualitative and Quantitative Methods

5. AVEs Are Not the Value of Communications

6. Social Media Can and Should Be Measured Consistently with Other Media Channels

7. Measurement and Evaluation Should Be Transparent, Consistent, and Valid

As much as I like this new focus, the Barcelona Principles are still not a framework, they simply provide guidance, which is why I don't believe they've been widely adopted. They make sense, yes, but acting on them is left up to individuals. That's not how most people change their behavior, however. Most need something that spells out much more clearly how they will actually measure the results of PR efforts.

AMEC's Integrated Evaluation Framework

Then, in 2016, along came AMEC's Integrated Evaluation Framework that puts the emphasis on setting objectives and measuring outcomes based on those objectives.[3] Its interactive version is a tool that provides more than just guidance. It's very intuitive and simple to use so that any new practitioner (or even a student) can follow the steps to plan, execute, measure, and report on a fully integrated communications campaign.

The framework spans through each PESO (paid, earned, shared, owned) channel and looks at the following points to get you to start planning your PR program (note, the order is important):

- *Objectives:* what you want to achieve for the organization and for your communication.
- *Inputs:* what you need in preparation for communication.

- *Activity:* things you do to plan and produce your communication.
- *Outputs:* what you put out that is received by target audiences.
- *Outtakes:* what your audiences take from and do with your communication.
- *Outcomes:* the effect that your communication has on audiences.
- *Impact:* the results that are caused, in full or in part, by your communication.

Now, some of those terms might be confusing, so AMEC helps us here, too, with a great taxonomy table that provides more information about those points, including key steps, metrics, milestones, examples, and methods of evaluation for each.[4]

The new AMEC framework is more than just a measurement tool; it's a planning and execution tool that makes you decide on the appropriate metrics and choose the right activities, outputs, outtakes, and so on before you begin any PR activities. It's a strategic tool to improving and measuring organizational performance, but it is quite vast and detailed for the day-to-day practitioner. Whether it will be widely adopted is yet to be seen.

In fact, very few PR firms today are seeing any growth from insights, measurement, and analytics according to the recent World PR Report by the Holmes Report.[5] That's a major concern for the PR industry.

As we can see, there are tools and frameworks that work, but why are they not accepted by the majority of PR professionals? Why do executives still devalue the necessity of PR because it can't be measured?

That, again, comes back to PR's inability to jump on the bandwagon, learn, and adapt to the new digital reality as quickly as their colleagues from marketing, advertising, sales, and so on.

Professor Watson confirms that this reluctance to embrace measurement is not new. "Despite the emphasis placed on measurement by the IPR in the U.K. and leading U.S. texts, many pre-1980 texts reveal great reluctance by practitioners to evaluate the outcomes of their activity." He adds that most PR people "faced with the difficulty and cost of evaluation, forget it and get on with the next job" (Watson 2011a, 8).

It's no surprise, then, that according to the 2016 Global Communications Report from the Holmes Report[6] current measurement models are still alarmingly focused on measures of outputs—such as total reach or total impressions—rather than on business outcomes. Agency and client-side respondents rated total reach as the most common form of measurement (68 percent), followed by impressions (65 percent) and content analysis (64 percent) with less emphasis on brand perception (47 percent) or attempts to measure return on investment (41 percent) and 30 percent still using advertising value equivalents.

Social media measurement is equally unsophisticated. The most common metric reported by agency and client-side respondents is a simple count of followers (78 percent), followed by reach (77 percent) and interactions such as likes or comments (76 percent). By comparison, relatively few are tracking sentiment (62 percent), social listening, such as real-time monitoring on conversations (47 percent) or changes in opinion or action (36 percent).

My favorite quote on PR measurement, though, is John Pavlik's comment from his PR research book saying that "measuring the effectiveness of PR has proved almost as elusive as finding the Holy Grail" (cited in Macnamara 2015, 2).

Each year, there are multiple studies done to research the PR industry. I'm not joking when I say that in each and every one measurement remains the biggest challenge for PR professionals again and again even though they all recognize it as absolutely necessary. Just take a look at the European

Communication Monitor,[7] CIPR's State of the Profession,[8] PRCA's Digital PR and Communications Report,[9] or PR Academy's Annual Qualifications Survey.[10]

This is still so puzzling to me, especially because precisely thanks to digital, PR can be measured. Practitioners simply need to use the tools that are there and they need to learn from inbound.

Inbound Marketing and Measurement

The inbound marketing methodology was developed with measurement in mind. Each phase within it has a particular goal that is *s*pecific, *m*easurable, *a*chievable, *r*ealistic, and *t*imely (SMART) and numeric:

- *Attract* is about turning strangers into visitors, hence creating traffic.
- *Convert* is about turning visitors into leads that we can nurture.
- *Close* is about closing those leads into customers.
- *Delight* is about retaining these customers to turn them into promoters to bring new customers to us or nurture their repeat purchases.

Each one of those can be measured numerically.

Not only that, the methodology also gives us the tools for each phase that can be used to achieve the goals.

- *Attract* uses SEO, keywords, blogging, and social media.
- *Convert* uses calls to action (CTAs) on blogs to bring visitors to forms on landing pages.
- *Close* uses customer relationship management (CRM) data to nurture the right leads through e-mail, marketing automation, or social selling.
- *Delight* uses surveys, social media, or contextual marketing (smart content) to offer even more valuable content.

To each tool and technique, we can assign tactical, numeric goals. For example, we can designate a number of visits and traffic for each blog or a particular conversion rate on a CTA so that we know that when visitors come to our landing pages, 25 percent of them or more will convert there and become leads with known e-mail addresses.

But the most important part of the methodology is that through marketing activities we affect the bottom line; we attract actual clients. Following the steps in the methodology, this is fairly easy to measure, and that's exactly what all businesses want: more revenue through new clients or more purchases.

The best way to plan your metrics and activities is to start backward:

- How much revenue do you need to make this year? How many customers/purchases does this translate to?
- Based on your close and sales activities, how many good leads or sales-qualified leads (SQLs) do you need?
- Based on the number of SQLs, how many leads in total do you need to ensure that you hit the SQL number (not all leads are going to be sales-ready or a good fit)?
- Based on the number of leads, how much traffic do you need to be generating?

These yearly numbers can then easily be converted into monthly goals and tactics, such as how many content offers you might need to put on landing pages, how many blog posts you need to publish per month, how many sales reps you need, how much social activity or paid advertising you should do, and so on. You can plan your entire marketing and sales (and PR) organization around this and everyone will know what their targets and goals are. This awareness makes it easy to consistently track and evaluate results to steadily improve.

The Future of PR Measurement

We know that lack or misunderstanding of data is a key challenge in digital marketing. A recent McKinsey C-level executive survey underscores that by placing lack of data as the second top challenge, after the lack of talent.[11]

The reason doesn't lie in the lack of tools or technology because we have plenty. The data is there. It's the approach that hinders this.

Regardless of whether you work in PR, marketing, or advertising, you need to start with the bottom line's goals in mind. That's what you measure against and that's what you plan your campaign, initiative, or activity for.

People will say that PR is not always measurable because it deals with relationships, emotions, connections, and reputation. Yes, these are qualitative and hard to measure, but you can always put them against bottom line goals. Why are you building these relationships? What exactly is this going to bring you? How many of your customers buy again from you because of your good reputation? Do you ask in your purchase process or forms what the reason is for them to come back again?

For example, crisis communications is a big area for PR. Here, the focus shouldn't be only about saving your organization's reputation but also looking into the number of customers lost or retained. Depending on the depth of the crisis you can even set a SMART goal against this and measure accordingly.

Once you have established the SMART goals that relate to your bottom line, you can dig deeper into the smaller, tactical objectives and expectations that can ameliorate the effects of a crisis. The idea is to put data and analytics at the center of everything you do.

We said that PR today deals with four different types of media. Let's look at some examples of how you can measure each one.

Earned Media

♦ Track referral traffic (use Google Analytics—it's free). Web analytics are hugely important in the digital era. You should evaluate how much referral traffic has come from media placements and how much from your own content, for example, owned media. Going deeper, you can track how many of those visitors have turned into leads, marketing-qualified leads (MQLs) or SQLs, and customers. Then, by knowing the lifetime value of your customer—how much revenue they bring you per year—you'll be able to easily calculate the ROI of those PR activities each month, each quarter, each year.

♦ Measure influencer relations referrals. If you are doing any type of influencer relations in which you partner with bloggers, YouTubers, Instagrammers, or other well-known influencers in the digital space that are relevant to your business, track how much traffic their stories about you have generated. Also, just as above, have you generated any customers from these activities and referrals? With influencer and media placements it's important that the media people you work with have links to your website in their stories, otherwise you won't be able to track any of this.

♦ Align with sales. Media placements are really good collateral for your sales team to use during the sales process because editorial stories or case studies are perceived as more credible than promotional content by your potential buyers. The question you need to answer here is: How can you ensure that you know when sales reps use any of this media collateral and what is the impact of the usage? The Sales Pro tools in HubSpot Sales can easily help you track this.

Shared Media

♦ Measure social media promotion. How many of your social media posts brought people back to your website?

How many of those converted on your forms? How many of those eventually became customers or media publishers?

♦ Evaluate social sharing. Is your social media community sharing your posts with peers or colleagues? This is an important indicator that tells you whether your content is worth remarking on.

♦ Track your total social reach. This will tell you how big your top of the funnel is on social media, which will give you an indication of how much more you need to grow it based on your overall goals.

Paid Media

♦ Measure paid conversions. I'm a firm believer that the best use of paid promotion is to set up ads that bring you conversions rather than just traffic or impressions. This goes back to the usage of Facebook, LinkedIn, or Google ads rather than TV or radio ads. Here you should look at how many of the people who saw your ads converted into leads that you can nurture and close as customers or media publishers. Again, this is an easy journey to track if you have the right goals set up and the right software to evaluate each step.

♦ Remarketing. This is another clever tactic that is easy to measure. Remarketing allows you to put targeted ads in front of people who have been at your website but have not become customers or publishers so you follow them around the web to encourage this.

Own Media

♦ Track organic traffic. How many people are finding you organically thanks to your content? How many of them are converting into leads, MQLs, SQLs, or customers? And how many of them are actually journalists or influencers who proactively reach out to work with you on a story?

Tracking these numbers will also give you an indication of your SEO and keywords ranking as well as insights into what you need to be doing more, for example blogging twice instead of once a week or building a designated subpage on your website for the media.

♦ Evaluate the most effective content. Figure out which blog posts have the highest call-to-action (CTA) clicks and which landing pages are converting best. This will tell you which topics you need to focus on as well as whether you've designed a good experience for your website visitors.

♦ Keep an eye on blog views and blog subscribers. This is another indication of whether your content is adding value for the people coming to your website, and the number should ideally be going up.

♦ Track domain authority and backlinks or inbound links. These are some of the main SEO factors. The more websites that are linking back to your content and website, the higher your domain authority and the better you will rank, because it means that your website is more trustworthy and relevant. And who doesn't want to be on the first page of a Google search? That's where searchers stay; they don't click through to page 10 to find you. They don't even go as far as page two. More backlinks and a higher domain authority, in turn, will improve your organic traffic and with that your organic lead generation, too.

♦ Assess average time on your website. How effective your website and content are is not just about the number of website visitors and conversions but also about how much time people who come to your website spend on it. This is easily tracked with Google Analytics, which also tracks your visitors from the first page they land on to all subsequent stops they make on other pages. In addition, this is a key metric for Google to rank websites.

Of course, these metrics need to be part of the appropriate report—daily, weekly, monthly, quarterly, or yearly. For example, high-level numbers like website visitors, leads, and total traffic conversion rates could be daily ones. Metrics related to blog views, blog subscribers, e-mail performance, inbound links, and rankings for one or two really important keywords could go into the weekly report. The monthly figures could include social reach, media referrals, landing page conversion rate, overall blog performance metrics, and traffic sources. For quarterly results, you might want to see what the most popular content has been for the last quarter as well as traffic source performance and organic ranking to make informed decisions about your activities for the next quarter. For the yearly report, you are also looking at these metrics to figure out the long-term effects of your efforts and to be able to plan strategically for the new year in terms of goals and then tactics.

One thing you'll see in the examples just noted is that none of them are vanity metrics such as followers, sentiment, or impressions. These don't really tell you anything unless you can very specifically tie them back to how they've boosted your bottom line. Vanity metrics are outputs not outcomes. Business owners and CEOs want the real numbers; they want actual proof of ROI, and the proof they often want is an increase in sales because it's measurable.

ROI for public relations, however, has always been difficult to demonstrate. When you add the inbound philosophy, it becomes possible; you know very well how your blog posts or media placements perform with regards to views and shares, the same goes for your landing pages and the conversion rates you get there. You know how many people open your e-mails and click on the links in them; you can track the entire journey of these website visitors and know when they become customers or publishers. What better way of proving the return on PR activities than tying each piece of content to a customer?

Using AMEC's Framework with Inbound

Let me give you a specific example here by applying the AMEC's framework and the inbound marketing methodology.

Objectives: What You Want to Achieve for the Organization and for Your Communication As just noted, CEOs want ROI, which basically means that they want more sales and revenue. Your objective, then, should be to influence or create an increase in sales for the organization. To break this down a bit, with inbound PR (which is highly digitally driven) your goal should be to deliver an agreed upon number of MQLs to the sales team, which will then close these leads into customers. To do this, you need to set objectives for all communication that you are going to do to get there, for example, a very specific number of visits generated through your website or the media's content, leads converted thanks to your e-books, referral traffic tied to media placements, and so forth. All of this is, of course, based on the number of MQLs you need.

Inputs: What You Need in Preparation for Communication In here, you need to have defined your target audience or buyer persona, as we'll explain later. Basically, who are those MQLs? What are their challenges, pain points, and goals? What are their demographic factors as well as behavioral attributes? How can you design your inbound PR activities to reach them with the content that they would be interested in and where they would find it? In addition, you also need a definition of an MQL that is agreed upon with the sales team, because each can have very different ideas of what an MQL needs to have done on your website or with your content to be a good fit for sales.

Activity: Things You Do to Plan and Produce Your Communication Knowing that you need to deliver a certain number of marketing qualified leads within a defined target audience, by when and in what frequency, here's where you plan your inbound PR campaigns and everything included in them to get to that number, organized around an appropriate time frame. Your entire strategic plan comes in here—your content plan based on your numeric goals, campaigns (e-books, media articles, events, surveys), e-mail marketing, basically everything around PESO that you need to do to achieve the objectives.

For example, this month you need 30 MQLs and you are starting from scratch so you need to first attract people to your website via the relevant PESO channels. These might include blogging and social media (owned and shared media) and influencer/blogger relations or some press releases and magazine pieces (earned media), then showing these people a call to action to lead them to a landing page where they will fill out a form with their contact details and become a contact in your database for the first time. After that you will engage further with them with more content and e-mails and, based on their response to those second and third touch points, you'll determine if they are qualified enough to be passed along to sales. (That was a simplified example, but it explains the thought process.)

Outputs: What You Put Out That Is Received by Target Audiences To analyze results, you need a clear picture of what you've done and all the tactics you have used. This is where you list all of these actions, for example, number of blog posts, e-mails, press releases, newsletters, social messages and so on. It's about the amount here rather than the quality or the effects. You still need to track these so that you know how much or how little you are doing so that next time you can plan better.

Outtakes: What Your Audiences Do with and Take Out of Your Communication Here's where you count things like visits, followers, shares, retweets, comments, subscribers, clicks and open rates. This is about how your audience has initially reacted and responded to your communication efforts. It's more about your top of the funnel growth rather than nurtured leads, but it's necessary to increase and maintain a large enough base because not everyone will be a good fit for your business (often, your top of the funnel contact database will include competitors or students, for example, who won't fit your target customer requirements to buy).

Outcomes: Effect That Your Communication Has on Your Audiences   Outcomes is where we learn what effect your inbound PR efforts have had on the audience. What you should be measuring here is increase in traffic and traffic sources, generated leads, best converting content offers or types and tactics, increased referral traffic from influencer relations, endorsements, number of actual MQLs generated, and how all of these metrics have developed week by week and month by month. Trends and insights are important as they allow you to make informed decisions about your next campaigns. This is why you need a holistic view of what's working to constantly measure, optimize, and get better.

Impact: The Results That Are Caused, in Full or in Part, by Your Communication   And here we solve for ROI. Did sales close some customers from those remarkable 30 MQLs we gave them? How can we link this back to the starting point of bringing people to the website through blogging and media relations, converting them into leads, nurturing them into MQLs, and passing them onto sales? Did any of those MQLs bring to us other MQLs through referrals and endorsements and thus improved our reputation?

   With inbound PR, PR is taking over a lot of the more traditional marketing activities but that's only natural and makes perfect sense—PR people excel at content and it is good, quality content that converts unknown visitors into leads. There are no good leads without good content. Nor are there any good relationships without added value.

To measure its results, PR needs to be aligned with sales. It's critical that everyone is on the same page and is working toward the same goals with a clearly defined funnel.

The future of PR measurement is practicing inbound PR because by using the inbound philosophy you start with the numbers that matter to the whole organization and only then do you plan your tactics.

Chapter 3

Inbound PR

Why You Need Inbound PR

When we think about what's happened over the past two decades, there are two key things to consider:

1. Our consumer and purchasing behaviors have changed, almost unrecognizably.
2. If you don't have an online presence, your brand doesn't exist.

Let's take a closer look at the first one.

The way we are influenced is very different today than it was a few decades ago. It's because we now have the power to let brands influence us or equally to not let them.

The process that we go through now to make decisions and buy products has fundamentally changed as well. We used to rely on direct sales and direct mail, TV and magazine ads, or media endorsements. Twenty to thirty years ago we didn't have the Internet; we couldn't really do much research on our own. We got our information from TV and the radio, and we relied on salespeople or the media to educate us on products as there was nowhere else to learn about new things or to find reviews. We also didn't need much convincing as the array of choice for products and services wasn't as extensive as it is today.

That's no longer the case.

We are a lot more sophisticated and empowered with hundreds of tools and technology. Essentially, our buying or decision-making process is a lot more conscious than ever before.

When we have a problem and need to solve it, the first thing we do is to go online and search for an answer. We go to Google or Facebook search, we type our problem, we check out websites, blogs, and brands. We check out vendors' social media presence; we chat to friends to get recommendations on social (even Facebook has this as a feature in the news feed); we dig deeper into specific brands and compare their offerings. And, oftentimes, we don't even need to speak to a salesperson, because we've done our due diligence and managed to convince ourselves on our own about what we need. Of course, if it's a bigger purchase, for example, an enterprise software decision, then we might rely on sales experts. Generally though, we educate ourselves through the content that we find, and we make our decisions on our own based on the content that we actively seek out.

Here's where the second key point comes into play. If I can't find your brand online when I'm doing my research to solve my problem, you basically don't exist. If you haven't used inbound PR or marketing to create and strengthen your own online presence as a business, I'm going to ignore you and ultimately not buy from you. I might even not find you to consider you in the first place.

In addition, we don't like when someone interrupts our research and content consumption process (like ads that we skip or fully disable). But we like to be engaged, enticed, and drawn into something interesting.

And that's what inbound is all about. It's about attracting people with the right, remarkable content that they would like to see when they need it.

Two decades ago, there were fewer journalists, fewer media outlets. Now there are thousands and thousands. Back then, the only way to get into the papers or on TV and radio was through the traditional media. Now you can use your own website for news and YouTube channel for airtime.

The Internet and social media completely changed the media landscape. They enabled a new era of two-way conversations where everyone can publish stories and reach a global audience in real time. This empowerment of individuals to have

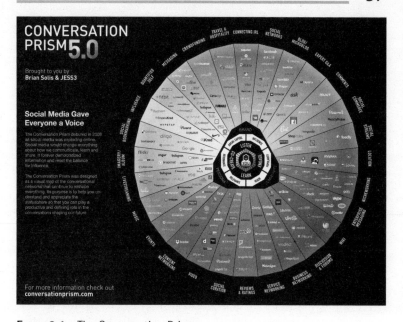

FIGURE 3.1 The Conversation Prism

Source: © 2008 Brian Solis (www.briansolis.com) and JESS3. Available for download at conversationprism.com.

their demands heard has led to a fundamental shift in how brands are expected to behave and communicate, online and off-line.

As Brian Solis's Conversation Prism illustrates so well, we are at the center of our own universe (see Figure 3.1). I am the most important person in my life. And brands have to catch up with me. Brian Solis calls this "Digital Darwinism," where digital moves faster than a company's ability to adapt.[1]

It's not just consumers anymore, though. Brands today have too many stakeholders and interest groups that build up a huge social graph. Employees, vendors, investors, and suppliers have become a lot more vocal. The media does not just consist of journalists anymore; it's bloggers, YouTubers, Instagrammers—all influencers that can have loud voices, big followings, and the ability to influence consumers and their behaviors.

To top this, anyone can be an influencer today. Think about Michelle Phan—a famous beauty vlogger (or YouTuber if you prefer) from Boston. When she was 17 she started with a personal makeup blog, then transitioned into doing YouTube makeup tutorials. She now has a highly influential voice with over 8 million subscribers, billions of views of her videos, and makes millions. Her net worth is $50 million because brands are killing it to work with her![2] And it all started just as a hobby.

Even journalists build their own brands; for example, in the autumn of 2016 Facebook started offering online courses for journalists that focus on three areas: discovering content, creating stories, and building an audience.[3]

The influencer landscape is not just immense but a driving force in today's digital era.

All the changes that have happened to society are also driving the world of business and how it needs to adapt. The same applies to PR and, as we've uncovered so far, some of the major reasons why PR needs to go inbound include:

- ◆ Consumer buying behavior has not only changed but is harder to influence.
- ◆ Brands need an online presence because otherwise they don't exist in the eyes of consumers or the media.
- ◆ There are so many influencers and stakeholder groups that traditional PR activities like press releases are not enough.

The changes in technology and consumer and influencer behaviors lead us to believe that traditional PR is outdated.

Outbound PR—in which PR practitioners simply draft press releases and e-mail them to their entire media list—doesn't work. Shift Communications, a PR agency that I'm a big fan of, did a research study using Google Analytics data and found that there were 1,092 press releases being sent every day.[4] That adds up to almost 400,000 press releases in 2016. But barely anyone clicks on them or reads them because they are not targeted.

What's more, with that many influencers out there, if PR people were to only do media relations, they wouldn't be able to reach the huge number of stakeholders and influencers—or publics—that we have today. No wonder PR people far out-number journalists. According to the U.S. Department of Labor, there are 4.6 PR professionals for every one journalist in the United States; according to a Canadian census, that ratio is 4.1 to 1, and according to a research study in the United Kingdom by the PRCA, the number is almost two PR pros for every one journalist.[5]

However, the one-to-one-to-many approach that was prevalent before, that is, the client-to-PR-person-to-all-journalists approach, no longer works because no one pays attention. There's too much noise to cut through.

The biggest reason why you should be doing inbound PR is that outbound PR interrupts. It's pushy and not relevant to our needs or experiences. But an inbound PR approach is because it attracts and is targeted to a specific stakeholder group. It's about being human-centered with content that is relevant, remarkable, and created for a specific audience and its needs.

The Inbound PR Concept

As mentioned, I come from a PR agency background. After three years in the industry, I was asked by HubSpot to join its agency consultants team in its Europe, Middle East, and Africa headquarters in Dublin, Ireland. It was a big move for me, not just personally by having to move from one country to another, but professionally as well by having to switch from one practice area to another.

Even though I was focusing on inbound marketing, I never lost my love for PR and continued researching and writing about it.

Working with over a hundred different agencies from across Europe during my first six months at HubSpot was eye-opening.

I realized that those coming from a PR background were doing very well with content creation but their colleagues from marketing, web, digital, or advertising were struggling with it.

On the other hand, PR people didn't fully grasp this "start with the numbers" inbound mentality. Their other counterparts had no issues with it because this is what they had always done—data had always stood at the center of their business.

So these two things—content and measurement—really got me thinking.

I then researched the different channels of the PESO model (paid, earned, shared, owned) and, as we've discussed so far, none of them work without good content. Content lies at the heart of all media channels and content creation is PR's real strength. But business results and ROI don't come without data, which is inbound marketing's real strength.

This got me thinking about what PR does and what inbound marketing does, and I simply connected the dots.

Inbound PR combines the best of two worlds (public relations and inbound marketing) and alleviates PR's biggest weakness (measurement) and inbound's biggest challenge (content).

What sets inbound PR apart from traditional PR is the ability to measure results.

PR has always been known for its inability to show the real ROI of its activities—you can't really tie a dollar value or a number of new customers to an article in a magazine. With inbound, quantifying efforts is possible; you know very well how your blog posts or online press releases perform with regards to views and shares. The same goes for your landing pages and the conversion rates you get there; you know how many people open your e-mails and click on the links in them. You can track the entire journey of those website visitors and know when they become customers. There are even ways to figure out how to bring people from press releases to your website and track them. What better way of proving the return on PR activities than tying each activity to a customer?

Having made this realization, I started experimenting with the concept. I began writing on my blog, LinkedIn, and Medium and people were responding positively. They were sharing and commenting that it makes sense. I was invited to write various guest posts for other blogs and publications. I was even invited to write a chapter for *#FuturePRoof*, which is a PR management book, a collection of the essays of over 30 global PR experts.

The moment it totally made sense that inbound PR was a thing was when my pitch to speak at INBOUND—the biggest inbound event in the world with more than 19,000 registered attendees in 2016—was accepted. I had spoken at quite a few other smaller events on the topic but when this talk finally happened, it was the ultimate success of inbound PR in practice. I used content to develop the concept; I used content to share it with the world through various PESO channels, including multiple events, which is a more of a traditional PR activity; and I used my HubSpot software portal to track everything. It's the ultimate application of my own inbound PR concept. And now you are reading its book.

In its very essence then, inbound PR is the combination of both practices—the inbound marketing methodology and traditional PR—and makes PR relevant again in our inbound world.

Benefits of the New Inbound PR Model

The main problem for brands today is the ability to stand out amid all the noise. The mass of information that's freely available and easily findable in the online space today pretty much has no end. Cutting through the information overload clutter is hard to do.

Drafting a press release, sending it to journalists via a mass e-mail, and expecting wide coverage can't help here. It's a myth of the past.

That doesn't mean you shouldn't be using press releases anymore or reaching out to journalists. It means that as a PR pro you need to adapt to the new world of content and online activity.

You need to focus less on the media and more on the publics, on the people that you want to reach—your stakeholders.

Then you need to use the tools, the channels, and the content formats that these people would actually like to find, read, watch, and then share.

This is the only way you can drive awareness and attract customers, the media, and other influencers. This way you can stand out and build lasting relationships with various publics.

If you are out there, you are searchable and findable; you are available and engageable.

Inbound PR gives you the whole arsenal of tools to do digital: blogs, social media, keywords and SEO, e-mail, landing pages, and so on.

By regularly writing and publishing on the various PESO channels, you use the power of your own content and own web presence to not just build but to own your reputation.

Creating your own news will drive inbound interest and traffic to your website. And if you have multiple content pieces that are remarkable, people will spend more time on your website wanting to learn more about you, downloading your e-books from your landing pages, and subscribing to your newsletter or social feeds. They will become genuinely interested in what you have to offer and the next time you send them an e-mail, they will actually open it, read it, and click on the link in it. If you do this right, they might even get in touch with you asking for your help. This not only applies to potential customers, but also to any type of media representatives—from newspaper journalists to influencers with their own blogs or

YouTube channels. In adopting this approach, you become your own media company.

Inbound PR is not just about using the media, it's about you doing your own PR with your own content on your own channels. You no longer need an intermediary to build your reputation because you can use your website, blog, and social media platforms to tell your stories and engage with people. The motto here is: have them find you rather than you chase them.

Pull versus Push

The biggest benefit of the inbound PR model is that you use pull rather than push. You attract people to you and your business with the right content, at the right time, on the right channel. You don't have to be the person who reaches out first with cold messages and pitches because with inbound PR you can create your own content machine and automatically pull stakeholders in with it 24/7.

The same applies to the media. Journalists now use online and social profiles to actively do research. In fact, social and mobile now dictate the journalistic craft. They use social to build their brands and find stories on their own. They don't need to wait to be pitched, and they don't want to. They hate e-mail pitches that look like spam—their inboxes are over-flowing (isn't yours, too?). So, do them a favor: have them find you. If you really want to get in touch with them, try Twitter or LinkedIn, if that's where they are active.

In addition, don't forget that journalists are not the only influencers today. Bloggers, celebrities, YouTubers, but also normal people can have huge social media networks and if your content is fascinating, if it's worth remarking on, they will share it. The word about you will spread via their messages, which become genuine endorsements of you, your content, your stories, your work, your business. There's no better sales pitch than other people's recommendations.

Next to building your organization's online brand with your own content on your own channels and letting new customers find you, you get to become a thought leader in your field and you strengthen your positioning. People know who you are and how much value you can offer them. They trust you. And trust is the best relationship-builder.

This will not only benefit your customer relations but also your media relations. Position yourself as an expert and thought leader, so the media will seek out your opinion and come to you, rather than you having to pitch them all the time. I call this inbound media relations (see Chapter 4).

As a PR professional who understands content, you can easily use all organizational materials, adjust them, and reuse them for inbound PR. Any informational piece can become an inbound content tool. Turn your press releases into blog posts, infographics, videos, white papers, and e-books, and use your own channels to promote them and generate leads and awareness.

Inbound PR is about educating people and helping them make decisions. If you offer them the right content in the right amount at the right time, they will end up choosing you.

It's one thing to create all that content, but it's another to put it in front of the right publics. Even if you have the best content in the world, without promotion it's not going to get you much traction. Inbound PR gives you all the channels to promote your content through blogs, e-mails, landing pages, social media, and so.

And getting to the nitty gritty, inbound PR allows you to track all of those activities and monitor how your content performs. You get the traffic and referrals, the conversion rates on your landing pages, you know how many visitors from your website become leads in your database (contacts that give you their e-mail addresses so that you can further engage with them) and you can also track how many of them turn into paying customers. Inbound PR enables you to measure the real ROI of your efforts.

PR people are good at content and engagement but lousy at measurement. The new inbound PR model is the solution. And it is the answer for PR agencies that struggle to remain relevant.

Why PR Agencies Need to Adopt Inbound PR

When asked what the world of PR will look like in five years, Iwona Sarachman, PR director at AmRest, said: "PR should reinvent itself; we are still rooted in conventional ways of thinking. If we don't do it, we will die out like dinosaurs" (Sarachman, 2016).

That's a scary thought.

But a valid one, because PR agencies have been known for not stepping up and owning new tools and technologies. They also haven't yet figured out how to disrupt the traditional PR business model where measurement has always been a challenge ("you can't quantify PR activities as they're all qualitative") and become data-driven agencies. PR pros today have unfortunately also been found to lack creativity, curiosity, and critical thinking.[6]

PR agencies (and agencies in general) always say that they don't have the time to invest in their own PR or marketing activities because they need to make their living out of advising and implementing such things for clients. This is a vicious circle, however.

Remember the questions from the Introduction? Let's go over them again:

♦ Do you blog?
♦ Do you use social media?
♦ Do you have a landing page on your site?
♦ How much time do you invest in doing PR for your own agency?

And again, you're probably asking yourself, "Why do I even need any of that? We have our clients, our team is busy, we can't invest time and money into something that won't bring us much result."

Yup, sure. For now you do. What about the future, though?

Far too often I hear, "We just didn't have time to blog this month, there's just so much going on with our clients." And I'd hear the same thing the next month and the next month.

Again, not having time for our own PR and marketing is one of the main challenges for PR agencies.

But this is the wrong way of thinking.

Why?

Because it's all about credibility. Why would I buy what you are trying to sell to me when I can't see you doing it successfully for yourself?

It's time to start practicing what you preach and become your own best client.

You need to become your own case study that you show to potential clients during pitches, and they'll be fascinated by your dedication to not only deliver this for other businesses but also do this for yourself.

It also builds trust. You want to create content for my business? If I don't see you creating content for your own business, then I don't believe you can create content for mine. It's that simple. Prospects and clients will trust you more because whatever you are offering them, you are using it for yourself, too, and following your own advice.

The best thing: if you want to try out new channels or experiment with some new tools or initiatives, do it for your own agency first to make sure it works before you do it for your client. You don't want to make major mistakes when you are working for clients, do you? Take the risk for your agency, not your client.

In addition, when you try things for yourself, you innovate. You develop new ideas and figure out new service packages or agency processes. In our fast-paced world you need to be constantly innovating to stay relevant and not die like a dinosaur. PR agencies are actually on that dangerous path, because according to the 2016 PRCA Digital PR and Communications Report, the main service that clients expect from them is still only media relations.[7] With inbound PR, we've discussed how PR covers all the PESO channels, but when you are not doing this on behalf of your own agency, no client is going to believe that you can do more than just media relations for them.

Especially when you are just starting out with inbound PR, building a case study with the results for your own agency is faster and easier than waiting to achieve this for your first potential inbound PR client.

It's time to challenge your thinking and behavior and to start doing what you tell your clients to do. Practice what you preach. This will not only drive more credibility and trust in your capabilities but also improve your client relationships and most importantly generate new business.

Be your own best client so that you can serve your clients best.

THREE KEY REASONS TO ADOPT INBOUND PR

If we look at what we've discussed so far, there are three main reasons why PR agencies need to adopt the inbound PR model.

1. Everything Is Digital   We live in a world where almost everything happens online. I've heard many people say that newspapers as we know them in their print version will disappear in 10 years. What does this mean for PR agencies? Well, you are going to have to go all in with digital and make it clear that PR is not just media relations.

Why this is not a reality already, I still can't fathom or explain. PR agencies are notoriously known for not being able to adapt quickly enough. This slowness happened once already—with social media. Even though it made perfect sense for the relationship-builders—the PR people—to own this space, it was advertising and SEO and marketing agencies that were quicker at jumping on the bandwagon, learning social and offering it to clients, and earning a bunch of PR awards.

Now a lot of this is happening again with digital. Digital and inbound are all about content. And who's great at content? Who's best at content? Well, PR. It's what PR people do. They are storytellers, they are writers, they can create remarkable content. Without remarkable content, no one will notice you anymore. There's way too much noise out there now and the fight for attention is tremendous. It's only with remarkable content that you can stand a chance. PR agencies, this is your way to the boardroom, your opportunity to show and prove how important you are.

And as the next disruption (artificial intelligence and robots[8]) is just around the corner, you better tackle the current one (digital) as soon as possible.

2. Measure It All   Measurement is the big debate in PR that has been going on forever. As we've discussed at length in Chapter 2, the majority of PR practitioners are still not measuring or evaluating the results of their work, even though there are plenty of tools and advice out there.

Many PR people are still using AVEs, although there are more than enough alternatives available. Even Meltwater—one of the well-known media monitoring software service providers—recently found itself in the middle of an online storm when it published a white paper fully supporting AVEs.[9]

It seems like it's too hard and complicated for PR people to make sense of all this and develop a system that's simple enough to be adopted.

What PR agencies need is a methodology that runs through the entire array of PR activities and aligns outputs with outcomes to measure results.

That's where inbound PR comes in. PR agencies can create a simple measurement framework to plan and measure each and every one of their actions based on overall organizational goals.

3. *Let Your Expertise Shine* There are hundreds of thousands of agencies out there and as we've explained, the barriers between marketing, PR, and advertising are blurring. The competition among agencies for winning clients is fierce. Not only that, traditional consulting firms such as McKinsey now fight for your clients by offering the same services, too.[10]

That's where the importance of agency positioning comes into play (see Chapter 5). Multiple studies have shown that clients want expert, not generalist, firms. They don't want an agency that promises everything to everybody—that's not very credible—they want real results from specialists who deeply understand their business.

With inbound PR, PR agencies can truly let their expertise—storytelling and relationship-building—shine because content is at the center of all inbound. It's remarkable content that attracts people to the business, turns visitors into leads, helps close them as customers, and ultimately drives results for the business.

Inbound PR lets PR agencies focus on what they are great at and capitalize on that expertise by creating remarkable content and measuring its results all the way through.

PR people understand how content works. They understand audiences, how they tick and what they need—whether customers or media. They understand the importance of relationships and how to drive them—whether on social or with the media. They understand how important a company's reputation is and can shape it since businesses often fail to that on their own.

Ultimately, inbound PR is about transforming an outdated agency business model and making it relevant again for the digital future. By being able to let your expertise shine and measure the results of all of your activities, you can create a repeatable business model for your agency and have clients come back for more, allowing you to drive recurring revenue and sustaining growth.

Chapter **4**

How to Do Inbound PR

The Inbound PR Methodology

As I was working on combining PR and inbound marketing, I thought there was a need for a visualization that explains the new inbound PR concept and how it relates to inbound marketing.

I decided to take the inbound marketing methodology and flip it into its inbound PR version (see Figure 4.1).

The inbound PR methodology can be applied to any stakeholder group: customers, clients, media, suppliers, employees, and so on.

Because media relations is still such a big area of focus for PR (and often not done well) and because we've found at HubSpot that media articles are, at 47 percent[1], the number one source after word-of-mouth that influences consumer behavior we are going to use the inbound PR methodology for the media in this chapter. Under media I include not just traditional media people such as newspaper, TV, and radio journalists but also bloggers, YouTubers, Instagrammers, and basically any influencer.

Applying the inbound PR methodology, what we want to do at the first stage—attract—is to bring the media to us. We do that by writing relevant content like blog posts, press releases, and social messages that are search engine optimized in order to be found. This is important because just as up to 80 percent of buyers make buying decisions without ever speaking to a sales rep, the media also use the power of Google and their networks to research stories and brands or influencers for them. Even if you pitch them, they'll come back and check out your online presence and if you don't have any relevant content, they are not going to consider you relevant, either. We continue to use press releases where relevant; used correctly, they remain the official instrument for communicating news.

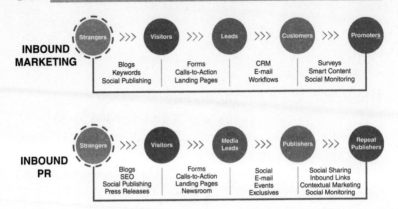

FIGURE 4.1   Inbound PR Methodology

Once we have attracted the media influencers to us, turning them from strangers to visitors, we want to entice them. We want to persuade them that we are relevant. We do that with even more, even better targeted content, which is often long form and thought out (either text or video). We include such long-form pieces gated behind forms on landing pages and ask the media person to fill out those forms so that we have their contact data and are able to reach out in a personalized, not mass pitch, way. This is how these people become our media leads and what the convert stage is all about. What we also do here is prepare a designated inbound PR newsroom that includes everything a media person needs to know and learn about us (explained in more detail later in this chapter).

We've managed to persuade the media how great we are with the remarkable content we have. We know exactly who they are and what they are interested in within our brand or business, so now it's time to reach out to them in a relevant and personalized way through social media or e-mail, based on their preferred method of communication. This is where we can offer events, exclusives, or anything special to seal the deal within the close stage. This is the pitch, where we turn our media leads into publishers. But I repeat, the relevant-only pitch—the right story material to the right media person. This is how we know it will really happen.

The last phase—delight—is all about relationship building. We've now worked with the media on some stories together, they've gone out, it's all been a win-win with some inbound links building; they link to our website, we link to their publication in our inbound PR newsroom. But we don't want this to be a one-off. We want repeat publishers. We should be thankful and use social to spread the word and share the work of the media people we've just collaborated with (not only the pieces that are about us but other interesting material they've created to show genuine interest). We need to be doing social monitoring to track what else they—and others—are saying and engage in those conversations that might spin up even more media opportunities for us.

We also need to ensure that we are using contextual marketing on our website (in the world of HubSpot we call this "smart content") so that when this same media person we've just worked with comes back, we give them additional and different information than what they saw the first time on our website. This is how we continue to add value with each new visit.

Now that we have covered the inbound PR methodology and its theory, it's time to get into the practical part.

How to Run an Inbound PR Campaign

When you are ready to put an inbound PR program in place and run campaigns, there are six key steps to follow to get you started.

Before you begin implementing these steps, though, make sure that you know what your or your client's goals are. We covered this extensively in Chapter 2, and you need those numbers to plan the following activities in terms of which ones you will use and in what amount, frequency, and so forth. The six steps to your inbound PR campaign are the tactics and the implementation that require objectives in the background in order to plan how much you need to do and to be able to measure as you go.

Let's look at what an inbound PR campaign needs.

STEP 1: NAIL YOUR STAKEHOLDER PERSONAS

The most important part is to define your stakeholder personas. With inbound marketing we speak about the buyer persona—the semifictional representation of your ideal client. It's who you are creating content for because you don't want to be found by just anyone, you want to be found by the right people who will buy from you.

We've already discussed how PR touches multiple stakeholders so this is why I use the word "stakeholder" here. The inbound PR methodology can be applied to any stakeholder persona. As with the explanation of the inbound PR methodology in the previous pages, we are going to focus on the media people and the influencers moving forward.

The first thing I used to teach my HubSpot agency partners when they started with us was to learn how to do research. I can't even tell you how many people gather data but merely rely on assumptions. And then they are not sure if whatever they are planning to do is going to work and get any resonance. In these cases, I ask them, have you interviewed or surveyed your personas? This is the time when it really hits them because they haven't.

If you don't do your research, you are not going to be able to make the right decisions that will bring the results you are seeking.

When doing your persona research, it's critical to develop a set of key questions to ask so that you can gather the right information.

I have that covered for you, don't worry. Let's take a look at a comparison between some typical buyer persona and media persona questions (see Table 4.1).

TABLE 4.1   Buyer versus Media Persona Questions

Buyer Persona	Media Persona
◆ Who are our ideal customers that are going to be interested in our content?	◆ Who are the journalists, bloggers, YouTubers, etc. that have an interest in us?
◆ What does a day in their life look like?	◆ What does a day in their life look like?
◆ How do they prefer to be reached?	◆ How do they prefer to be contacted?
◆ How do they do research when making a buying decision?	◆ How do they do research when picking and writing a story?
◆ What are they looking for when making buying decisions and what do they worry about?	◆ What are they looking for when working on a story and what do they cover exactly in their stories?
◆ What challenges do they face when making buying decisions?	◆ What challenges do they face when working on a story?

What we need to know is who are the journalists and influencers that might have an interest in us based on the stories that they write, the topics that they cover, and the brands that they've already worked with? What does a day in their life look like? Are they very busy in an office where the phone is ringing the whole time, or do they write in a small coffee shop? How do they prefer to be contacted—with thousands of press releases a day being sent out, e-mail might not be the best vehicle. They might prefer Twitter or LinkedIn. Knowing what a day in their life looks like will give you hints, too. If the office is busy and loud they probably wouldn't want to have a conversation there as it would be too stressful and distracting.

We also need to know what their decision-making and research processes look like when they are preparing and writing a story. Do they go online and visit websites or do they go to events? What exactly are they looking for in a story— maybe facts and data or maybe interviews with executives and prominent people? What challenges do they face when they are working on a story? Perhaps they have a very short lead time and only have one day to submit their story. This is important to know as it will allow you to be flexible enough to help them with such a deadline.

Developing a clearly defined stakeholder persona is at the center of inbound PR. It's the key piece that drives everything else, and without it none of the following steps will bring the desired results.

To define any of your stakeholder personas, you need to start with researching your stakeholder base, analyzing your current website visitors or media placement outlets; talking to your sales, marketing, and HR people; and ideally conducting interviews and surveys with your existing and potential stakeholder personas.

The Key Stakeholder Persona Research Questions
Whichever stakeholder persona you choose, it all boils down to the following questions:

- Who are these people?
- Are these people really the people we want to be doing business with (in whatever capacity)?
- Who exactly are they and what are they like (demographic information, job level and seniority, hobbies, and so on)?
- What does their day look like?
- What questions are they asking?
- What are their goals?
- What are their pain points?
- What are their challenges?
- What is it that they are looking for when making decisions?
- Where do they go for information to make these decisions?

By answering these questions, you'll be able to develop a clear picture of the audience you are hoping to reach. To really do so, your persona should drive each and every piece of content you create and each and every activity you undertake.

STEP 2: DEFINE YOUR STAKEHOLDER JOURNEY

After developing your personas, you need to define their entire decision-making process—stakeholder journey—to ensure that you are creating content that answers their questions at the right time.

When we speak about customers, we have the buyer's journey, which is the active process each of your buyer personas goes through from being a stranger to becoming a customer. There are three stages: awareness (of a problem), consideration (of potential solutions), and decision (to buy from you or work with you)

Let's focus on our media persona again. Here we want to illustrate the process that they go through to make the decision to work with us on a story.

At awareness, our media personas realize that they need to write a story. They usually have some timelines as well. At consideration, they evaluate ideas, angles, and specifics about the potential story. At the end is decision where, after all the research, our media personas pick the brands and influencers to complete their story.

For each of the stakeholder journey stages you need different types of content because your persona asks different questions at each stage (see Table 4.2). The idea is that you

TABLE 4.2　Stakeholder Journey

	Awareness	Consideration	Decision
Buyer Persona	I have a problem.	I'm researching solutions.	I'm picking a brand or the top solution to solve my problem.
Media Persona	I need to write a story.	I'm researching topics.	I'm picking my story and brands or influencers for it.

provide relevant answers that build up in a logical way and gradually become more product-, service-, or brand-focused.

- ◆ *Awareness* is about attracting and educating, it's about providing helpful content that is easy to consume and share. Think short e-books, infographics, checklists, press releases.
- ◆ *Consideration* is about providing solutions to the identified problems at awareness with content of higher value. Longer e-books, research findings, webinars, or case studies and success stories work well here.
- ◆ *Decision* is about you and why you are a better choice. This is the stage where people are ready to make a final decision. Product trials, demonstrations, consultations, assessments, interviews, and exclusives are good options.

As you know by now, it is content that drives everything within inbound—but only the right content. Content must be relevant both to your personas and your business and should gently guide them to choosing you. This is why mapping out the stakeholder journey is so essential before you develop the content.

STEP 3: CREATE A CONTENT PLAN

Having defined our personas and their decision-making journey we can now create the content that is needed to support this process.

The way to go about creating this content plan is pretty straightforward, but believe me, it's done the other way around by so many PR and marketing professionals. Often, they come up with a few topics, write some blog posts about them, and hope for leads after perhaps adding some content offers gated behind landing pages based on the blogs that perform best. This is a very wrong way to go about it.

The only way to create content that is going to convert is to start with the persona, then to define the key questions the

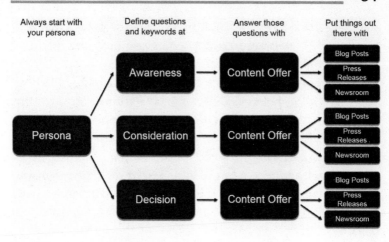

FIGURE 4.2 Content Plan

persona is asking at each of the stages of the journey (see Figure 4.2). Once you have these questions, I always recommend starting with just one for each of the decision-making journey stages. Being focused is key here. When we have one key question it's time to think about how we are going to turn this into a content offer to gate behind a form on a landing page—an e-book, a quiz, some research, a video interview, a live webinar, and so on. Then we are going to think about how we need to promote these content offers and brainstorm the ideas for the blog posts, the press releases, or any other materials we publish—these play the role of promotion pieces for the content offer. We do this once, and the second time around (maybe the next month), we return to our key questions and pick the next stage.

Depending on your stakeholder persona, the end goal of inbound PR would be to generate customers or secure media placements. The further someone goes into the decision-making journey, the more personalized and targeted the content and the touch points should become.

When working on your content plan, it's not just about blog posts, it's about creating different pieces of content that suit the particular decision-making journey stage and gating that content behind a landing page where people must provide their contact details to get it.

This is how you generate leads. It's an exchange of value; you offer your visitors high-quality, educational, newsworthy, and timely content, they recognize its value and are willing to fill out the form and give you their e-mail address, name, and other information in exchange for it.

For each content offer, plan at least two blog posts with calls to action to promote it, multiple social media posts, as well as nurturing e-mails or newsletters. Ideally, you want to have a content offer for each of the stages of the decision-making journey to create a holistic campaign that answers all the questions your persona has.

STEP 4: PROMOTE YOUR CONTENT

Great, you now have truly remarkable content created and published. It's time to make sure it reaches your audience.

Among marketers, there's a misunderstanding that all you need to do is build the content and people will come. Even with the best SEO machine, you still need to heavily promote your content to drive traffic and engage with your stakeholders.

The challenge here is that we are surrounded by a ton of information everywhere. There's just way too much noise.

Many of my HubSpot agency partners would create fantastic content and then share it on Facebook once, on Twitter once, and on LinkedIn once. And that's about it. Then they would tell me, no one is reading our blog.

But you need to promote your posts multiple times on various channels in different ways. The life of a tweet is less than 20 minutes so, of course, not everyone is going to see your wonderful content.[2] Put it out there properly and they will.

To help you with this content promotion piece, I recommend using the PESO model by SpinSucks—probably my favorite PR agency in the world (see Figure 4.3).

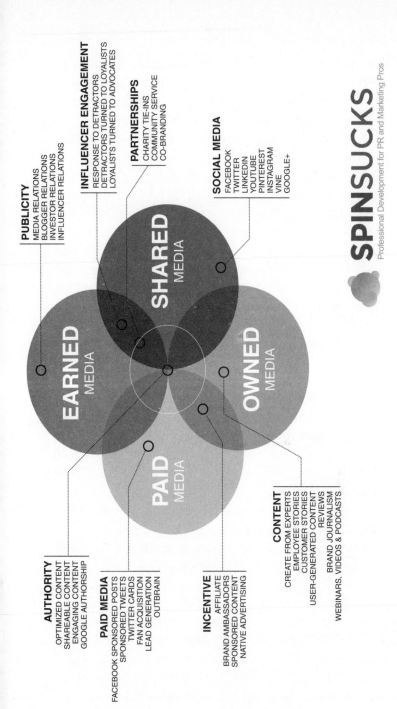

PUBLICITY
MEDIA RELATIONS
BLOGGER RELATIONS
INVESTOR RELATIONS
INFLUENCER RELATIONS

INFLUENCER ENGAGEMENT
RESPONSE TO DETRACTORS
DETRACTORS TURNED TO LOYALISTS
LOYALISTS TURNED TO ADVOCATES

PARTNERSHIPS
CHARITY TIE-INS
COMMUNITY SERVICE
CO-BRANDING

SOCIAL MEDIA
FACEBOOK
TWITTER
LINKEDIN
YOUTUBE
PINTEREST
INSTAGRAM
VINE
GOOGLE+

AUTHORITY
OPTIMIZED CONTENT
SHAREABLE CONTENT
ENGAGING CONTENT
GOOGLE AUTHORSHIP

PAID MEDIA
FACEBOOK SPONSORED POSTS
SPONSORED TWEETS
TWITTER CARDS
FAN ACQUISITION
LEAD GENERATION
OUTBRAIN

INCENTIVE
AFFILIATE
BRAND AMBASSADORS
SPONSORED CONTENT
NATIVE ADVERTISING

CONTENT
CREATE FROM EXPERTS
EMPLOYEE STORIES
CUSTOMER STORIES
USER-GENERATED CONTENT
REVIEWS
BRAND JOURNALISM
WEBINARS, VIDEOS & PODCASTS

EARNED MEDIA

SHARED MEDIA

OWNED MEDIA

PAID MEDIA

SPINSUCKS
Professional Development for PR and Marketing Pros

FIGURE 4.3 PESO Model
Source: © SpinSucks.

63

We've already discussed the four different types of media but what this illustration gives us are more ideas about how to promote our content in a structured way. It's important to use all of the media types to achieve the desired results.

Let me give you a quick example. If we start with earned, let's do some blogger relations. Then let's maybe experiment with some other social networks like Instagram. With owned, let's repurpose the research into a quick video. Then let's push that video with some Facebook sponsored posts or native advertising. There you have it.

Don't stop at just sharing your blog posts or content once after you publish it. Good content starts performing and ranking a month after publication. Schedule some social media posts for the future and make sure you leverage your evergreen content on an ongoing basis. Fresh content is fantastic but don't forget that you already have some remarkable content pieces that you can repurpose and share again. This can easily become an inbound PR service offering that gives you quick wins and optimizes time, efficiencies, and resources.

Finally, don't make the mistake of just sharing your blog posts. Promote your landing pages that gate your content offers directly.

STEP 5: NURTURE YOUR LEADS

The beauty of developing content for each of the stages of the stakeholder journey is that you can use them to create personalized e-mails to engage further with your leads. This is called marketing automation or e-mail drip campaigns.

For example, someone stumbles upon an awareness stage blog post on your website, they click on the call to action to your landing page, they like the white paper that you have as a content offer on it, so they fill out the form sharing their e-mail address with you, and they become a lead in your contacts database.

You wouldn't want to stop there. This person is clearly interested, so now is the chance to nurture him or her further through the decision-making journey with personalized e-mails that offer more valuable content such as consideration stage blog posts or content offers until you get him or her to the decision stage. After that, you continue to delight him with more advanced and educational content.

Having followed the content plan method I explained, you'll be far more strategic, not just in terms of your content creation but also your marketing automation efforts because you'll already have content that logically builds upon itself to continuously add value until your persona is persuaded by you.

Content is the fuel for lead nurturing. With such a personalized approach as marketing automation, you can measure very precisely what works and what does not.

The same approach we use to nurture our prospects into clients can be applied to the media persona as well. By having figured out their journey and creating content based on it, you can design automated e-mail drip campaigns and help them move to decision by showing respect, care, and relevancy. Or you can even use the relevant stage content with social media if that's their preferred communication vehicle.

With some strategy behind this, media lead nurturing can do wonders for you, because your media prospects will remember your personalized manner and clever use of technology.

Step 6: Measure Results

We've discussed that one of the biggest PR challenges is measuring results. With inbound PR, you can not only drive tangible results, but also track them.

With good software in place or with a good combination of a few tools, you can see what sources are driving the most traffic (organic, social, paid, and so forth), how well your landing pages are converting, what your e-mail open and click rates are, and how many customers you are generating from their first touch point with you until the last.

Being able to measure the effectiveness of your activities allows you to continuously optimize and improve, and justify the time and effort spent doing inbound PR.

It all comes down to just using the data.

I'm shocked at how many PR people don't focus on it. There are so many free tools out there—take Google Analytics for traffic; Hootsuite for social monitoring and management; the HubSpot CRM for contacts and lead management; Coverage Book to create great reports with your company mentions. It's all there! Record the data at least on a monthly basis, analyze it, and make informed decisions based on what's worked and what hasn't. This is all about getting in the habit of doing an evaluation on an ongoing basis and sticking with it.

Also, plan with outcomes in mind, not outputs. What is it that you want to achieve rather than writing five press releases, sending them to 500 journalists, and then showing the three media clippings that you got out of this to your client.

Always start with the numbers and by numbers I mean objectives. We covered this at length in Chapter 2, but it's essential to know why you are doing what you are doing because this is what you evaluate against.

Your key learning here is to measure against your goals from the very beginning and continuously optimize as well as adjust the goals based on the data if needed. This is what smart business thinking and decision making is all about.

Inbound Media Relations

In the previous chapter, I mentioned that earned media is part of the promotion piece, so let's take a look at it in a bit more detail.

The reason why I want to spend a whole chapter on media relations is twofold. People generally think that the only thing that PR people do is media relations, and, admittedly, the majority of PR agencies still only do media relations. Currently, however, media relations is done in a very outbound way—it's untargeted, not personalized, and pushy. Mass press release pitching needs to become a thing of the past.

Since the media hasn't gone away and because consumers heavily rely on the opinions of influencers, it all comes down to credibility, so you as a PR person will sometimes still need to rely on intermediaries to tell your stories and news for this added credibility.

This is why it's important to figure out how to do media relations better.

Here's my model for doing media relations the inbound way.

STEP 1: DO YOUR RESEARCH FIRST

Just as with your own business, you need to be strategic with your media outreach. You need to do your research in order to make informed decisions and create a plan for successful media relations with the right influencers and outlets.

Journalists and other influencers are highly active online. They use the Internet and social media to stay up-to-date, research and write stories, and also to build their own personal brands. Some have their own blogs, others guest blog or leave thoughtful comments and maintain strong social media presences. In fact, 56 percent admit that they cannot perform their normal duties without social media.[3] So, for them it's not just about listening but also about sharing their opinions and thoughts and promoting their content.

This is all great news for you. The very first thing you need to do before you send your story to the media is to heavily research the media. You don't want to send your story to just anyone because that's not going to get you any coverage. You want to send it to the people who would actually be interested in your content. Please, do your research first—stalk those journalists, influencers, and media outlets online.

Read what they write (news coverage, blog posts, or any previous pieces), follow the conversations they are in (on

LinkedIn groups, in Twitter chats), just get to know them—their interests, their pain points, their challenges, the things that they are working on. If your story solves one of those challenges, well, then you have a win-win situation; you help the journalist, and the journalist helps you, too, by spreading the story.

Target the right media people just as you would target the right buyers for your products. You have a much better chance for your content or press release to get picked up that way because it will spark genuine interest.

So, don't waste your influencer's time, value it. And personalize the experience—show that you've done your research, show that you know what they write about, what they are interested in, what their pain points and challenges are, and how you can help solve them with your story or news.

STEP 2: GET CREATIVE WITH YOUR OUTREACH APPROACH

How many e-mails do you receive daily? If you work in a fast-paced industry, I would say hundreds. For journalists, bloggers, and other influencers this number is probably in the thousands. That's a lot of e-mails. The worst thing is, probably 90 percent of all those e-mails are completely irrelevant pitches that simply go into the spam box.

To give you the actual numbers from 2016, journalists in the United States received an average of 1,092 press releases every single day. Barely any of those got opened.[4]

Having done your research first, you will have identified the media people who would be interested in your story and won't consider it to be spam. But to make sure the story reaches them, e-mail might not be the best option, because media people get bombarded with irrelevant pitches.

As mentioned, journalists are active on social media and mobile. They definitely understand how digital, real-time communication works, so why not tweet them or message them on LinkedIn? Just send a brief message to see if they would be interested and have the time for you. Go with the channels they use and the way they prefer to be approached. Through your initial research you will have found that out.

Step 3: Don't Be Spammy and Don't Overdo It

Within your outreach, make sure you don't do too much. Don't send your content or reach out to the same person again and again and again. Maybe send one reminder, but if you don't get a reply, then the individual is not interested. Journalists are busy and so are influencers. Respect that. And stop trying because it's irritating. Maybe they'll remember that gesture and they'll come back to you one day. Either way, don't waste their time and don't waste yours, either. Don't overdo it. If they are interested, they'll get back to you. If not, don't be a spammer. Move on.

Step 4: Create Remarkable Content

I can't stress this enough: good content is the fuel of inbound PR. If you are thinking about writing a press release, instead of just using simple text, how about turning it into an infographic or a video graphic? Try to stand out and come up with something that hasn't been done before. It will get you noticed.

I'll give you a great example. A few years ago, The Corner Shop PR, a London-based PR and marketing agency, sent the launch press release for the upcoming *Charlie and the Chocolate Factory* musical (directed by Oscar-winning Sam Mendes) to journalists on a USB stick shaped like a Wonka-branded chocolate bar.[5]

Journalists were thrilled and they shared their excitement about the clever pitch idea on their social media profiles, simultaneously increasing the buzz around the musical.

Let influencers remark on your content.

You see, even with this rather traditional PR tactic—a press release—you can use inbound to pull the media in and get them excited, instead of pushing me-too messages again and again. If your content is good, journalists and bloggers will include it in their stories and they'll link back to your website. That will get more people to it and build up your SEO authority.

STEP 5: USE EMOTION IN YOUR STORIES, NOT SO MUCH STRUCTURE

Yes, the inverted pyramid and the who, what, when, where, why, and how are important even in your own blog pieces, not just press releases, but is that the approach you capture hearts and minds with?

We are emotional creatures, we make decisions based on feelings, so don't be boring. Entice the media people, challenge them, involve them, make them want more. A perfectly planned and organized piece that follows a strict structure would probably not succeed at that. Be different, be bold.

Indeed, press releases are important as they are still the official instrument for communicating news but being different and unorthodox is what allows you to stand out. For example, why not get out of the box with videos or social cleverness?

Also, be different with your e-mail and social media out-reach, too. Make your messaging stand out by bringing up the pain points and challenges of those media people and relate them back to your story. Highlight the "what's in it for me" angle and refrain from only speaking about you, your client or brand, and products. Make it about them. Turn them or their readers into the heroes of your stories.

STEP 6: DON'T FORGET YOUR OWN CONTENT AND CHANNELS

I just have to get back to this again. Say you have a great story. You write the press release. You follow the suggestions I just discussed. A journalist picks it up and finds it interesting. But the journalist is not just going to copy and paste it and publish it. Just as you do, journalists do their research first. They'll check your website, your blog, and your social media channels to see if you are real and credible. If there's nothing going on there, they'll move on. They'll have questions and you should have answers to them with your own content. Why? Because this will save you and the journalist so much time. For example, how about being bold and getting your leadership involved in this story, too? Have them publish their version, their point of view on this story on your corporate blog or on their personal LinkedIn. Try to make them experts and thought leaders, give them a voice in the online space. Journalists will come asking for their opinions, so give them some good quotes even before they have asked for them.

Speaking of your own channels, don't forget the social media profile buttons that lead to your social media accounts. Place them everywhere, making it easy for journalists to find your social presence. Media people are busy; they don't have the time to google your company's Facebook page—and why should they bother? It's happened to me so many times. I go to a company's page, I like what I see, I want to check them out on Facebook and reach out via Messenger, but links and buttons are nowhere to be found or don't function. I could go to Facebook and Google and find the page, but this is completely destroying my experience. I'm sure you know what I'm talking about. Don't be that company.

Step 7: Make It Easy for Journalists to Get in Touch with You

It's also important that once you've successfully attracted media influencers to your website you make it easy for them to reach the right person when they need to discuss a story. Have a media contact listed there, not just an empty form they need to fill out without any idea about who is going to see the request and respond to it (if at all).

There will be situations when journalists and influencers will want to speak to you. Maybe they want to expand the story, maybe they want to run multiple interviews. Regardless, you need to make sure your website has a press page that includes your media relations contact information, some company statistics, recent coverage, and other materials that might be useful resources for the media. Speaking of contact information, this should be the contact information for a real person, why not with an image of what that person looks like—this changes the experience so much, it sets expectations for journalists, too, about who they are speaking to.

STEP 8: SHARE THEIR CONTENT

The story is out. It's great, it's about you. The journalist or blogger will promote it, the media outlet or blog will, also and you should, too. But don't stop there. It's not just about spreading awareness about yourself and how great your story is, it's about continuous engagement.

The idea here is not just to spread the word about you, but you should also make sure you mention the journalist, blogger, or influencer and the media outlet. You show your appreciation, and it's a nice gesture because you are supporting the writer's reputation, getting her more traffic and potentially more followers. Good deeds get remembered.

Soon that influencer might come to you for more because you've had the courtesy to say thank you by promoting her work and she wants to reciprocate. You can build some great relationships that way, and you are helping them, too, because more than 75 percent of journalists feel more pressure now to think about their story's potential to get shared on social networks.[6] Sharing their content shouldn't end with the stories they've written about you. Engage with other content pieces they've created, too—share, retweet, comment, favorite. Just have a conversation, it's a two-way street.

Think about the delight section of the inbound PR methodology—it's all about long-term relationships, not just immediate gains.

The Inbound PR Newsroom

Any company that does inbound or focuses on content marketing inevitably ends up with lots of content—press releases,

FAQs, research papers, other resources, and various materials that are all over the website and so become hard to find.

This is why I always advise my agency partners to have a resources page within the menu of their website where they put all the important e-books, guides, videos, white papers, podcasts, links to social sites, and other content in one place. As time goes by, they create more and more content that gets scattered all over their websites, but having such a resource page puts all the important information right there for potential customers to find and engage with.

This is important for your buyer persona. But if we review the inbound methodology and think about media relations and our media persona, the one thing very few companies do is to create such a resource section specifically designed to help the media easily find the information they need about you for their stories. I call this the inbound PR newsroom.

Basically, an inbound PR newsroom is the media's go-to resource. It's how you convert the media influencers from people potentially interested in you to people who want to work with you. It's something you can offer as a service to build for your clients as well as create for your own agency.

Unfortunately, only 6 percent of journalists feel that digital newsrooms meet their expectations.[7]

Indeed, while researching a number of newsrooms, the only ones that I found to be well developed, were those of very big companies.

Red Bull, for example, has a designated website called Red Bull Content Pool with lots of content that journalists can search through when they are working on a story.[8] It includes global news, latest events and productions, editorial highlights, featured media rooms, search function, and more.

Coca-Cola also does a great job with its press center that has a whole library of press releases, images, company articles, infographics, and contacts throughout the globe (see Figure 4.4).

Figure 4.4   Coca-Cola Newsroom

Source: www.coca-colacompany.com/press-center.

To give you some B2B examples, take a look at Lenovo's news website.[9] It has a logical structure with a very clear menu that consists of the six most important areas: news/stories, investor relations, blogs, multimedia, press kits, and resources. Every one of those areas breaks down into relevant subsections so that you can easily find what you need.

My absolute favorite example is Cisco's newsroom. You can spend hours there learning about the company's initiatives, vision for the future, culture, leadership team, global growth, and more and engaging with its content and social channels (see Figure 4.5).

Having an online newsroom is a fantastic way to ensure that you are doing media relations the inbound way so that you can attract, convert, close, and delight the media and encourage them to come back again and again.

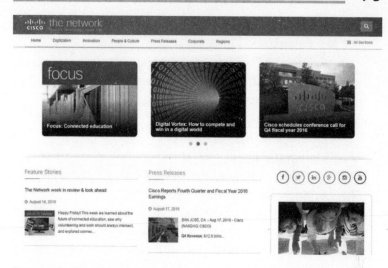

FIGURE 4.5   Cisco Newsroom
Source: https://newsroom.cisco.com/home.

To fully meet the media's expectations, I want to show you what you need to have in your inbound PR newsroom. It's a simple 16-step formula.

16 Key Things Your Inbound PR Newsroom Needs

1. Recent media coverage
2. Press releases—current and archived that can be sorted by year, product/service, topic, and so on
3. Bylined or guest/contributed pieces for other magazines or blogs
4. Research or studies and white papers that can also be sorted
5. Product/service information, fact sheets, and guides
6. High-quality visual materials such as images, logos, or videos in different sizes and formats
7. Case studies and testimonials

8. Interviews or videos with important people from your company

9. Events and speaking engagements (of prominent people at the company)—past and future so that visitors know where you are going to be

10. Podcasts and webinars (with presentation slides, maybe a SlideShare feed)

11. Online media kit with company history and FAQs

12. Executive bios and their or company awards

13. Investor and financial information

14. Contact details to make it easy for the media to get in touch with the right person at your organization (even PR contacts for after hours in case of an emergency)

15. Blog feed and social profiles links and a Twitter feed

16. Search and sort functions as well as subscribe options for the media to follow what's happening in the newsroom

Here are three important tips when you are working on creating or optimizing your newsroom:

1. Make sure you have a logical and easy to use newsroom architecture. Based on research, almost 95 percent of journalists visit a company's website at least once a month and 41 percent of them search for information on a corporate website at least once a day.[10] Make each and every one of their visits remarkable. This happens by carefully planning things like menus, subsections, and above-the-fold information. The 16 things I mentioned that belong in your newsroom comprise a lot of information, which is why it's important to spend plenty of time thinking about how you combine all of these resources and where you put each item in your newsroom.

2. Update and optimize your newsroom regularly. Treat it as part of your own PR. No one wants to see a blog that was last updated a year ago. It's exactly the same with your newsroom; it's supposed to be a living representation of what's going on in and with your company.

3. The same thing applies to regularly updating your media contacts. Update their e-mail addresses or phone numbers as soon as they change. You'd be surprised how often this gets overlooked. If a media representative wants to speak to you, he or she wants to speak to you now. Don't waste his time.

Today, it's all about the user experience or the media experience. It's the experience that you design for journalists, bloggers, YouTubers, or influencers that makes or breaks your inbound PR newsroom and your relationship with them.

An inbound PR newsroom can be a good fit not just for big companies but also for smaller businesses that want to get noticed or have their SEO improved by developing targeted content.

How to Create Fascinating Content

We've seen how content rules our world.

In the digital era, content is the most important asset a business can have. It's no longer your product or your service, it's the content you create about it (and around it) that gets you found and noticed.

Even though we are surrounded by so much information (and noise), people always want more. But they want quality over quantity. They want you to guide them and teach them. They want you to solve their problems. They want you to give them solutions. And they want to have fun. Everything we've discussed in the previous chapters is dependent on content.

So what exactly is the content that you need to create to stand out?

The demand generation is hungry for so-called remarkable content: content that is worth consuming and sharing, content that shows WIIFM (what's in it for me?), and content that fascinates.

That type of content should be the fuel of your inbound PR efforts so that you can connect with your audience and distinguish yourself to avoid being just the next me-too business, product, or service among the million others.

There are three essential steps you need to follow to create compelling content for your inbound PR purposes.

Step 1: Know Your Stakeholder Personas

The first and perhaps most important step to creating fascinating content is knowing who you are creating the content for. Who is going to consume it? Who is going to be interested in it? Are those people really the people you want to be doing business with? What are they like? What questions are they asking? What are their goals? What are their challenges? What is it that they are looking for?

Stakeholder personas help you decide how and where to focus your time and effort to attract the people you want as well as to create content that is actually helpful, content that solves exactly the problems that your personas have, content that answers their questions.

It's not just about content, content, content; it's about the right content. You don't want to be found by anyone, you want to be found by the right people. For that to happen you need to create content that is relevant to your personas and to your business. You need to dig deeper and ask questions. Stakeholder personas should be at the center of all of your activities. They should guide each and every piece of content you create, including small things like your tweets.

STEP 2: MAP YOUR CONTENT WITH THE DECISION-MAKING JOURNEY OF YOUR PERSONA

Now that you've defined your stakeholder personas, it's time to analyze the questions that they are asking and create a logical path to answer them at the right time. Why is this important? Because your stakeholder personas ask many questions, but not all at the same time—some people are already aware that your products exist and are more interested in knowing about the benefits. Others have no clue yet that your product or service could be a potential solution to their problem; they are only searching for more information about the existing alternatives. Or they may not even realize that they have a problem, which is your chance to grab their attention.

As we've discussed, the stakeholder journey is the active process each of your personas goes through from being a stranger to your brand to becoming a customer or deciding to work with you. For each of the three stages—awareness, consideration, decision—you need different types of content. It can't be too much; it needs to fit with the knowledge and needs of your personas.

At awareness you want to attract attention and educate. At consideration you want to go deeper and provide solutions. At decision you want to convince that it is you who is the best. This is the first time your brand name gets mentioned, it is where you have earned the right to speak about why you are better because you have already educated your readers. You've given them possible solutions to consider and so by guiding them you've earned their trust in you as an expert. And now you have built a relationship that has captured hearts and minds. Here's where you tackle and address any objections they might have.

The basic idea behind the decision-making journey is to give your personas a series of interrelated interactions and content that gradually increase in relevance and resonance. At each stage, people ask different questions that progressively add up and become more product- or service-focused. You need to offer them the logical next step to move them further along in their journeys. Your audience's needs and expectations take priority.

A useful exercise here is to put yourself in your persona's shoes and see things through her eyes: You've got a problem—let's say you want to start going to the gym, but you've never done it before. Obviously, there are some things you need to consider. Which gym and where? Should you get a personal trainer or sign up for classes, and so on? You start your research with some general questions and discover more, you even find out that you might need some fitness gear, clothes, and sports shoes.

Because you have some issues with your ankles, you are now aware that you need good sports shoes with great support. You have defined your problem, the *why* is there, so now it's time for the *how*—finding the right type of shoes or your solution.

You start researching more about the different types of shoes—for training, for running, for various other sports, with extra cushioning, with awesome breathing technology, and more. You discover that you need stability shoes that prevent your ankles from rolling inward. Now it's time to find the best product and so you start comparing stability shoes of different brands, individual product ratings, and customer reviews. You weigh the pros and cons, check out the prices, perhaps even the design, and you make your decision—yes, you want to have Nikes.

Great! You now have the decision-making journey defined, what's next is to start thinking about the different content you need to be creating at each stage to gently guide your persona to make the decision to choose you. Emphasis here is on the word "gently"—you cannot push people; we are far too sophisticated and educated now to even pay attention to pushy advertising.

Mapping out how you can answer these questions at each stage is essentially your content strategy.

Content marketing is not ad hoc. You can't just create content whenever you find some time or inspiration and a trendy topic to newsjack. You need a solid plan based on informed decisions made when researching your personas and the stages of their decision-making journeys.

Content without strategy doesn't lead to long-term success. Only carefully planned activities help build long-lasting relationships that lead to customers and customer loyalty.

STEP 3: USE FASCINATION TRIGGERS

Now that you have your content plan and strategy in place—you know your stakeholder personas and have mapped out their decision-making journeys—you can get to the nitty-gritty of actually creating the content.

For many businesses, this is the most challenging part: how do you create content that stands out among all the noise? How do you capture attention with so many distractions? Our average attention span today is shorter than that of a goldfish: only eight seconds.[11]

Exactly because there is so much information available out there, you need to spend some time figuring out how you can distinguish yourself and your content, attract people, and earn their interest.

One option is to use fascination triggers to make your content and stories even more powerful and engaging.

This is not something I just made up but is based on research, namely, the Kelton Fascination Study,[12] which was the first-ever marketing research study specifically focused on how people and brands become more fascinating. It identified seven main facets to fascination: innovation, passion, power, prestige, trust, mystique, and alert.

Sally Hogshead, who facilitated the research and is the author of the best-selling *Fascinate: Your 7 Triggers to*

Persuasion and Captivation (Hogshead, 2010), explains that when your audience is in a state of fascination, they're more likely to buy from you. They're more likely to like you, trust you, believe you, and follow you. They're more likely to post about you on social media. They return to you for more because you're adding intense value through this focus.

By using fascination triggers you tap into people's emotions. You connect with them on a deeper level that goes beyond just providing them with information. You affect their feelings and moods, and so their behaviors. You build a relationship not just trigger a one-off transaction.

The guiding principle here is: Solve for your reader's mind, but compel for your reader's heart.

Here's how you can use the seven fascination advantage triggers in your content and inbound PR activities.

Innovation   Change the game with creativity and surprise people by always getting to the next level. Red Bull is perhaps the best brand at this type of storytelling, considering all their stunts—Red Bull Stratos[13] is by far my favorite.

Passion   Connect with emotion and excite people by making use of the different senses. Great example here are the food blogs packed with amazing pictures of delicious food and step-by-step photo recipes that make your mouth water.

Power   Lead with confidence and be a thought leader. Cisco is doing a fantastic job here with its #InternetOfEverything content that is innovative, compelling, and data-driven, encouraging you to learn more and persuading you to trust Cisco's expertise.[14]

Prestige   Earn respect with higher standards and demonstrate that you are better. Hierarchy and rank are obviously great symbols to tap into here, but sometimes humor works, too, as in the car war between Mercedes and Jaguar.[15]

Trust Build loyalty with consistency and commitment to solve problems. Lufthansa and its #inspiredby, in which the airline shows people's amazing experiences and journeys around the world, is a great example of how to create reliability through storytelling.[16]

Mystique Communicate with substance and don't overdo it. Arousing curiosity here is your goal—check out Siemens' The Helping Hand.[17]

Alert Prevent problems with care, but create some urgency around them first. Fear is a good emotion to use here just as the Speed Ad Mistakes viral video did.[18]

Summing up, the one big learning here is that inbound PR is about building relationships. This doesn't happen overnight. It takes time, energy, effort, and consistency. It also requires that you have done your research and developed a strategy that allows you to make informed decisions based on your stakeholder personas, their decision-making journeys, and how you can fascinate them with the right content at the right time, triggering the right emotion. Using such triggers can be the perfect basis for effective storytelling that captures your readers' hearts and minds.

The Art of Inbound Storytelling

Everywhere I turn nowadays, I see how powerful and sophisticated ordinary people have become, how they really own what they want to hear, see, touch, and experience.

This is the reason why outbound and the world of push messages is dying. Quickly.

For PR pros and marketers that's a big deal, especially for those still used to the old techniques like TV, radio, direct mail, ads, and mass media pitching. I'm not saying these don't exist anymore, they are just not that relevant or effective.

One example comes from a research study by Fractl and Moz, which found that more than 54 percent of people don't click on ads and 58 percent use ad blockers.[19] So advertising (push messages) is not an effective way to attract people to your business. What is effective is offering content that people are truly interested in. For example, 55 percent of consumers are more likely to buy from you if they like your story.[20]

Why is that? Because this type of content is relevant; because these are stories that we want to hear, we want to make them part of our lives. Only through them do we allow brands to speak to us. Yes, I say "allow" because we can now make that choice. It's within our power. It's only what truly attracts us that we consciously choose to pay attention to.

More so than ever, businesses need to be innovative and clever with their communications approaches to reach and deeply engage their audiences, because it's a noisy, fast-paced world out there.

Even a robot-generated print newspaper that is curated almost entirely by algorithms based on social-sharing activity and other user behavior is coming to market.[21]

So, if this is the future of the media and considering that PR has always been about influencing organizational audiences and particularly the media, how can PR influence robots?

Well, it can't.

But it can influence that social-sharing activity and behavior of readers. How? By harnessing the power of storytelling.

Gary Vaynerchuk (whom I'm a big fan of) says that the one thing that binds us together, regardless of our professions and backgrounds, are the stories we tell.[22] That is never going to change because great storytelling is the way we make real money, real impact, and real change. And there's a very simple reason behind this: we are all human beings, and we've relied on storytelling since our species began. But the majority of organizations and professionals are telling stories like it's 2007 in a 2017 world.

The big challenge today is to tell a story in micro moments at the right time on the right platform. Our everyday life is based on the notion of time famine—we are always busy, we never have time, so we never really sit down and focus on a particular piece. We just continue to scroll down and consume as much as we can as fast as we can.

In addition, we increasingly control how and when we choose to consume or not to consume content. We have devices that let us skip ads, shows, or news and select what it is that we want to watch or read and ignore what we don't want to pay attention to.

Time is our most important—and rarest—asset.

This means that capturing the attention of audiences has become close to impossible.

We are therefore experiencing a culture shift in digital story-telling called "breaking news storytelling." To get people's ears and eyes where you want them to be, you need to act quickly, basing the content on people's actions, behavior, and interests.

To win the fight for attention you need inbound storytelling that spans through all of your inbound PR activities.

Whether you need more visitors on your website, more media placements, more influencer relations campaigns, more leads, more social followers, or more customers—it all comes down to telling good stories that engage your audience and make them trust you and buy from you or do business with you.

There are six key factors for effective inbound storytelling.

1. KNOW YOUR STAKEHOLDER PERSONAS INSIDE-OUT

You need to understand the pain points and the challenges of your audience. You need to speak to their needs and desires in their language and solve their problems. Only then will your stories be relevant. They will be about a real issue that your audience is familiar with or has experienced, and they will offer a solution to it. Your content will be helpful and what better way to build trust than by helping?

(Do you see how I repeat stakeholder personas more or less in every chapter? Yes, they are that important!)

2. Discover Your Brand Story

As Simon Sinek says, it's not about what you do or how you do it, it's about why you do it.[23] Why do you exist? Besides money, what makes you tick as a business? Your brand story forms the backbone of all of your communication. Find out what makes you unique. That vision and mission should guide your entire storytelling.

3. It's about Them, Not You

Incorporating your brand story into your storytelling doesn't mean only talking about yourself, your business, and your products. Learn to stop doing that. No one is listening to it. People are only interested in themselves and their problems or needs. According to research presented in the Brand Storytelling Report 2015, 66 percent want to hear stories about regular people, only 10 percent might want to hear about the CEO's or founder's story.[24] Get comfortable seeing things from their perspective, not yours. Again, be helpful. It'll come back to you.

4. Be Emotional and Make Them Feel Something

The stories that engage are the ones that touch us emotionally, they make us feel something—happiness, anger, surprise. Be creative and use your people skills to appeal to your audience on a deeper level. Make them feel part of the story or help them fit into it in a special way. Make them care. Capture their hearts and their minds. Use the fascination triggers mentioned in the previous pages to achieve this.

5. Be Consistent and True to Your Brand Story

Coming up with one amazing story that resonates with your personas and differentiates you is probably not going to cut it. Your content strategy needs to be ongoing and consistent. It all adds up and creates a journey of stories that people should be able to experience at any touch point with your brand.

6. Use Storytelling in All of Your Communication Formats
I've mentioned native advertising and sponsored posts as part of paid media. These tactics can still be effective, but only if you make them relevant and engaging, turning them into enticing stories rather than push messages. The point I'm making here is that you need to apply storytelling to all of your inbound PR efforts—your blog posts, your social media messages, your press releases, your videos, your e-mails, your case studies, your social advertising posts, and so on.

Inbound storytelling engages people; it captures their hearts. It makes them remember you—you stay in their minds and when they are ready, they'll come back to you again.

The key learning here is that inbound stories make people take action.

The Five-Step Storytelling Model
To create such a powerful story, you need to follow a five-step model that includes:

1. A reason for the story to be told.
2. A hero as the main character and other protagonists such as the enemy, the victim, the supporter.
3. A conflict that the story starts with and that needs to be resolved such as tragedy, journey, hunt, romance.
4. Emotions that are evoked as the story evolves such as surprise, joy, love, fear, anger, shame, grief, disgust.
5. Viral power to spread across all PESO channels.

This is the model that designs breakthrough storytelling.[25]

The inbound PR stories of the future are slowly moving away from text, information giving, and announcements to images, emotion sharing, and video stories—often in real time.

Chapter 5

Generating New Business with Inbound PR

Practicing What You Preach

As a PR agency or communications team, how much time do you spend building your own organization's profile with your own content? Many would say "none" or "barely any" but in the digital age, this is unacceptable. And isn't this what you ask clients, too? Isn't trying to convince them that they need to build their online profile with content what you are selling?

Also, why are you asking clients things like "Do you need a new, sustainable way to drive people to your business and attract clients?" "Do you struggle being seen as a credible and authoritative brand within your industry?" "Are your current methods not bringing the right results?" to figure out how they differentiate themselves but not asking yourself about these things or choosing to ignore them?

When it comes to you—the communications expert—you fail in communicating about yourself.

Yes, doing PR and marketing for yourself requires time, effort, and commitment, but it works, just as it does for clients or customers. And because PR people are storytellers and content creators at heart, practicing inbound PR for themselves could quickly become natural because they are doing it for clients already.

Much of this may be more relevant to agencies; however, all of these practices can apply to internal communications teams. For example, your internal team wants executive buy-in for a new social media campaign for a new product. Show them how social media campaigns work for you and have driven tangible results.

I've said this before but I'll repeat it: it's time to start practicing what you preach and become your own best client.

A simple reason is that marketing spend by professional service firms highly correlates with the firm's revenue growth rates.

So, the next time you are making the excuse that you don't have the time, just block off a Friday afternoon when clients are not ringing and work on a simple PR campaign, draft a press release, and put it on the news section on your website so that journalists can find it. Create a short e-book that would be helpful for your potential buyers and publish it on a landing page to generate some leads. Don't stop there, though. Write a blog post about your e-book and share on social media. In addition, publish a blog post about that press release, but use more accessible language to share the story and your perspective as well as why it should matter to your readers and customers, what's in it for them, and why they should care about it.

Notice something here? It's about them, not you.

Yes, it's still your content and your channels, but focus on the benefits for them: your customers, your readers, the influencers.

Bear this in mind when we speak about media here: a journalist's role is not to promote you, your business, and your products, it's to write a great story that will get read by the right audience and that fits with their media outlet. Respect that. Give journalists what they need, not what you need and want.

When you are creating content for your own channels, make sure you speak the same language as your audience and are on the same level. Don't try to impress with pompous or highly technical words. Be relevant and resonate with the language your audience uses every day. Make it easy for them to consume and understand what you are saying.

Why is this so important?

Because information and education are powerful. They are the primary decision-making and purchase drivers in the digital economy.

Today, you inform and educate with content. You empower with your storytelling, and you become a thought leader with dedication and consistency for valuable content.

As a PR practitioner, you use the skills of storytelling and writing to make you stand out among the other professions. If you are not telling your own stories on your own channels how do you expect me as a client to trust that you can do that for me?

Sure, case studies and customer testimonials are great but isn't it mastery and dedication to do well yourself that impresses the most?

Potential clients also check you out. When they are researching vendors or service providers they will look for content on your website and assess it. If there's barely anything there, they are not even going to want to speak to you.

To top this, experimenting on clients is the worst thing you can do. If you want to try a new tactic, a software program, or a tool, try it yourself first before you recommend it to someone else. If you do otherwise, you risk harming the client relationship, losing trust, and potentially facing some bad reviews that won't do much for your reputation.

This is especially true if you are just starting to build your digital and inbound capabilities. You can't start offering new services without first thoroughly testing them, because no client will feel confident that you can actually deliver. You need to walk the talk.

If you want to see how others do it, I have three truly great examples of agencies that treat themselves as their own clients, with appropriate budget, people responsible for their own marketing and PR, and a communications plan:

1. *Arment Dietrich*. I'm a huge fan of this Chicago-based PR agency that has fully adopted the PESO model on behalf of itself. You'll see it in the sheer amount of content that they create. Check out their blog at www .spinsucks.com.

2. *PR 20/20.* This is the very first PR agency to move to inbound marketing and add inbound services. It's had a 180-degree transformation. Its story is powerful and I definitely recommend checking it out: www.pr2020 .com/story/history.

3. *Square2Marketing.* These guys are the masters of inbound marketing. Not a PR agency but a true example of practicing what they preach. If you are interested in adding metrics and inbound into your services, read everything on this company's website: www.square2marketing.com.

When I look at the pages and the blog posts of these three agencies, I am filled with confidence that if I were to buy services from them, they would be able to deliver. That's the stage that you want to get to as well because this is the basis for generating new business with inbound PR.

It's not just the vision, it's the masterful delivery and you being your own proof of it.

The Importance of Positioning

I spent a good three years working in PR and digital agencies across Germany and the United Kingdom. After that, as a Principal I Channel Consultant at HubSpot, I was on the other side and my role was to help our partner agencies grow their businesses.

This not only included teaching them the inbound marketing methodology and how they can use our software for their own marketing, but also offering them strategic advice on how to choose the right market; develop and deliver better services; recognize areas for growth; make the right team decisions in terms of hiring, training, or management and leadership; establish expertise; and more. So I was doing a lot of business consulting.

In my previous jobs, I always thought that agency life was hard (and it is, don't get me wrong), but I've now seen that running an agency isn't easy, either.

Especially when you have to compete with thousands of other similar firms out there.

From what I've experienced, one of the biggest challenges agencies face is developing a unique positioning that allows them to truly stand out and be seen as an expert, with clients chasing them for their knowledge and capabilities, rather than the agencies having to pitch all the time for new business.

While an exact number is difficult to quantify, one source estimated that there are over 560,000 agencies in the world—from advertising to design to marketing research and PR.[1]

Now it's time to ask yourself: Which one are you? And most importantly, what makes you unique?

If we line you up next to all other agencies out there, how will you stand out?

It doesn't matter when you say you are a PR agency. The lines between marketing, PR, and advertising are heavily blurring in the digital space. Especially when agencies fail to communicate their positioning.

About two years ago, I held the first-ever HubSpot Partner Classroom Training in London on the topic of agency positioning strategy. HubSpot Classroom Trainings are one-day training sessions, usually on topics such as marketing automation or content creation but are not agency-related.

When I was preparing for the day, I reviewed the websites of the partner agencies that were attending and copied their positioning statements (I had to translate some from various languages into English). One of the first slides that I showed them at the beginning of the training day included these statements without saying to whom they belonged. I then asked them: What do these statements have in common?

Silence.

Then they figured it out: "Oh, that's us."

The shock, though, was that they all sounded the same.

As a potential client reading these statements, I wouldn't really know which one to choose. They were not making it easy for me.

However, a few hours later after diving into some practical activities, all partner agencies had a breakthrough experience.

We looked at their ideal clients, buyer personas, and target markets. The result: all were completely different. But there was zero clear communication on their websites, on their blogs, in their content, or in their social media accounts. There was nothing to show that differentiation.

Positioning is hard. It's hard to define, it's hard to make the choice to stick to it, and it's hard to live by it consistently.

But it's necessary because if you want to run a sustainable agency business, you need to be able to stand out and be seen as an expert in a particular field. You need to be able to tell the story of how different you are and the unique value you provide.

Otherwise why would I choose you among the 560,000 other agencies out there?

Positioning allows you to do exactly that—it's about making the choice about what services you offer and which markets or customer segments you serve and then clearly communicating that choice externally.

Sounds easy, right? Not always.

The main issue is fear of focus. Many agencies believe that if they choose a niche, a specialty, a particular industry, or simply something narrower, they will be limiting themselves and missing out on potential revenue.

However, it's simply not possible for you to be everything to everybody and be excellent at absolutely everything.

By trying to appeal to everybody, you end up appealing to nobody. In the long run, this is not a sustainable strategy; it's actually not a strategy at all. One-size-fits-all is basically one-size-fits-none.

Here are the five key benefits of a strong agency positioning strategy.

1. Clear Direction Externally and Internally

Your team, your current clients, and your potential clients know what you do, whom you do it for, and how you do it. Everyone is aligned, everyone is on the same page; you know where you are going and how to get there.

This is very important internally because it helps with decision making when situations arise that cause you to think: "Oh, here's this new potential client, totally different from everyone else. We've never done anything like this before and they want this and this and this, and so we should put a lot of effort and time and go outside our area of expertise, hire someone, and add that service to somehow make it happen."

2. Saving Yourself Time and Money Qualifying

When you have a clear profile of your ideal client (buyer persona), you can create targeted content on your website, blog, and landing pages to attract the right leads—only the clients you want to work with.

This helps you solve the issue of appealing to everyone because with a quick look at your homepage and the rest of your content, potential clients will be able to decide for themselves whether you're right for them or not. This way you allow them to self-qualify themselves and you won't be wasting your time (and money) chasing the wrong leads.

3. Giving Clients What They Want

What do you think is key for clients when choosing among the 560,000 agencies out there?

Expertise.

In fact, 72 percent of businesses are more likely to buy from thought leaders, people or businesses that are recognized as experts in their markets.[2]

No client ever wants to buy a wide range of expertise, rather they look for specific expertise that fits with their needs.

Clients are selfish, they want the best for themselves. They want world-class specialists with unique, valid, and reliable capabilities and knowledge that will help them grow their businesses. Most importantly, these are capabilities and skills that the client alone cannot acquire internally or take in-house, whether due to talent or resources.

In his blog, Blair Enns, author of *The Win Without Pitching Manifesto*, puts it best: "A design firm that specializes in branding is like a fish that specializes in swimming. It's not a specialization, it's the cost of entry. And 'full service advertising agency' has always been the language of a small generalist trying to look like a big generalist" (Enns, 2015).

Not full-service generalists, but focused, specialized agencies are the ones gaining ground—a trend that has been increasing over the past decade in all agency rankings.

Here's an extreme, but no-nonsense example of how clients think and how you should be seeing it, too:[3] "Would you want a dermatologist performing open heart surgery? I hope the answer here is 'no.' . . . You wouldn't trust a dentist to stitch up a wound, either, so why are you trusting a catch-all PR professional to cover your intricate and complex industry?"

4. CHARGING MORE FOR YOUR SERVICES

As we've seen in the previous point, clients want expertise and insights, not just some generic information on how to market their products or services that they can get from any of the 560,000 agencies in the world.

With specialized knowledge built around a particular service, tool, or market segment, you become the expert, the only one among all the competition who knows this best.

By being the only expert in that field, you can charge more for your services. You have the power in the client-agency buying relationship because clients have little choice.

Bear in mind the words of Blair Enns in his book *The Win Without Pitching Manifesto* that the goal of positioning should be to reduce the viable number of competitors to your firm and shift the balance of power in the buy-sell relationship from the client back to you (Enns, 2014).

The power of the client is not money, but choice—the ability to choose among 560,000 agencies out there.

And why do I keep saying "560,000 around the world"? You might be thinking "Well, that's worldwide, I'm based in the United States." I'd answer: "So what? The world is global—with the Internet, and Skype, and Zoom, location is often irrelevant today (unless you specialize in local knowledge, which can be a differentiator)."

5. BEING ABLE TO SAY "NO" AND CHOOSING TO SAY "NO"

One of the key long-term success factors for agencies is the ability to say "no" to the wrong clients—both prospective and existing ones.

If you are aligned with the previous four benefits, then this one should be easy. At the end of the day, you don't want to be working with companies that don't have the budget or the willingness to grow, or those that don't trust your expertise and want it done their way. These clients are not worth your time or effort—they are not a good fit and they are not ready to trust and rely on you.

Excellence comes from saying "no" internally, too—either to the wrong employees who don't believe in and follow your vision, or in situations where you are considering adding a new capability or scratching a service that you are not great at and doesn't make you stand out. It's better to focus on your strengths and build upon them instead of wasting time on areas where you are weak.

Ultimately, by developing a strong positioning strategy, you'll be able to escape the sea of sameness. As Tim Williams, author of *Positioning for Professionals*, says, "Most agencies are swimming in overserved markets, offering common services, but hoping to make uncommon profits," instead of uncovering and developing the solutions clients will need tomorrow.[4]

Instead of swimming into the red ocean of same-space competition among 560,000 agencies, with a strong positioning strategy you'll be able to swim into the uncharted waters of the blue ocean, where few are swimming.

It doesn't stop with identifying your positioning, though. You need to live and breathe it. And you need to practice it. The content that you create, the events that you speak at, and the inbound PR activities that you use for yourself need to be fully aligned with your positioning.

This is how you'll be able to develop content that adds value. By communicating your positioning and putting it front and center as your biggest strength you are not just the next me-too, you are different, you are you. You are one of a kind. You do not purport to be great at everything, trying to satisfy any need. You are extraordinary at one particular thing, and you do it better, faster, stronger, more efficiently than others because you are focused only on that; you are the very best at satisfying that one need.

People will know you as the expert in that area, and they will refer others to you because you have stood out and stuck in their mind. You've earned their interest and you've convinced them that they should pay attention to you in the oversupply of undifferentiated agencies. You've become a thought leader.

THE 11 PROCLAMATIONS TO WIN

Having nailed your positioning makes it possible for you to follow the proclamations that Blair Enns identifies in *The Win Without Pitching Manifesto* (Enns, 2014), which, as the name says, encourages agencies that sell ideas and advice to ditch the pitch mentality and regain the trusted agency-client relationship with professionalism and respect both ways:

1. Specialize because expertise, not personality, process, or price, is the only valid basis for differentiation against competition and allows agencies to deal with clients from a position of power; when you specialize, the client will have fewer alternatives to hire someone else and a decreased ability to dictate the terms of the relationship.

2. Replace presentations with conversations by ditching the need for a big reveal in the win-or-lose situation of pitching; through conversation both parties discover whether they would be a good fit to work together whereas the presentation is just one-sided.

3. Diagnose before prescribing by digging into the systems and asking why five times, because clients need an external perspective to see problems differently.

4. Rethink what it means to sell by turning selling into change management and helping people solve their problems; capitalize on this facilitation of change rather than talking people into doing things they don't need to do.

5. Do with words what you used to do with paper by charging for ideas even when they are spoken, not only when they are in the written proposal.

6. Be selective when picking clients so that you can find perfect fits and say no to those who aren't; in doing so, build credibility and expertise.

7. Build expertise rapidly through identifying problems and solving them, writing to deepen the expertise and artistry to put it out, and by documenting this process to refine and improve it continuously.

8. Don't solve problems before you are paid by cherishing your thinking and ideas as your highest value product because otherwise clients won't, either.

9. Address issues of money early to avoid clients who can't pay; for clients to be a good fit they need to be a financial fit, too.

10. Charge more as your expertise deepens and the impact on your clients' businesses grows to reflect that impact, because price premiums allow you to invest in your agency, people, and company to grow even more, too.

11. Hold your heads high as professional practitioners who seek respect above money, because when you are respected as experts the money will come in anyway and be used by you to become even better.

The agencies that follow these proclamations are "reclaiming the high ground in the client relationship, beating back the pitch and winning new business without first having to part with their thinking for free. . . . They have gone from order-taker suppliers to expert advisors and have forged a more satisfying and lucrative way of getting and doing business" (Enns, 2016).

To get there, let's develop a strong positioning strategy to drive everything that you do.

How to Create Your Agency's Positioning Strategy

Having gone through why positioning is so important, now you are probably asking, "How do I create such a strategy? I've never done this nor can I hire one of those fancy consultants to help with it. I don't have a process to follow here."

Inspired by Tim Williams' book *Positioning for Professionals* (2010), I took on the challenge of developing a very simple process for creating an agency's positioning strategy that has been implemented at HubSpot.

Ideally, you would want to block off almost a full day to work on this if you want to do it right, and you want to involve your people at the latter steps as well. Positioning is a team effort because everyone needs to buy into it. Otherwise, you won't succeed at establishing your positioning externally.

Get yourself a Word or a Google document and start writing while following the seven steps next.

STEP 1: DO A BRIEF AUDIT OF YOUR CURRENT POSITIONING

Take a few moments to think about whether you've ever gone through a formal process of creating a positioning strategy for your agency. What were the results? Does this still apply today? Does it still work?

If you haven't gone through such a process, that's okay, too. Take a look at your website, blog, and social media platforms as well as your sales pitches; check out your business plan and business strategy documents. Based on this quick audit, write in one or two sentences what differentiates you and where you stand at the moment.

This doesn't have to be perfect (but we'll get there, that's what we're doing here). Just spend a few moments thinking about who you are now and how you communicate this externally.

STEP 2: DEFINE YOUR WHY

Remember Simon Sinek's talk "Start with Why—How Great Leaders Inspire Action?" If you haven't seen it, watch it now![5]

There's a powerful statement in it that's going to stick in your mind forever: "People don't buy what you do, they buy why you do it."

The *why* is your reason for existence.

Think about how you can answer the following questions:

- Besides profits, why does your agency exist?
- What problems do you solve and why?

- What would you like to achieve as an organization, if you knew you could never fail?
- If your people were volunteers instead of employees, what would they be volunteering for?
- What would happen if your agency ceased to exist tomorrow?

Some of those questions are tricky. They're tough. But they are important. I always recommend that the CEO or the agency owner work on them because they have to do with the agency's envisioned future.

Step 3: Define Your Who

The purpose of a positioning strategy is to state that your agency is right for some clients but not all clients. You can't be everything to everyone.

This is why it's important to define your agency's buyer persona—your best-fit clients, the ones you want to be doing business with in the future. Use the following questions to define them:

- What types of clients have you been most successful with in the past?
- What traits do they have in common?
- Which industries, business categories, or market segments do you know best and excel at serving?
- What are the businesses that seek out your help the most?
- What types of clients do you not want to do business with? (What traits do they have in common?)

Failing to identify your buyer personas results in a one-size-fits-all strategy, which really is a one-size-fits-none because by trying to appeal to everybody, you end up appealing to nobody.

Knowing who your best clients are will help you to say no to the wrong ones and by communicating that best-fit client profile on your website, potential clients will be able to recognize on their own when they are not a good fit for your agency.

STEP 4: DEFINE YOUR WHAT

Clients want experts. They want thought leaders. To become a thought leader, you need to build expertise in a particular field. You do that by focusing on your strengths and building upon them, not by expanding your services to fake it or trying to fix your weaknesses so that you can sell the client engagement. You simply can't be excellent at everything.

This is why it's important to identify your core competencies—those key abilities that you are really great at and that bring economic value to your clients, and, as such, to you, too.

Think about the services and the products that you offer and then answer these five questions:

- Do you want to be hired for what you do (production, delivery, supply) or what you know (strategic ideas and advisory)?
- What do you do particularly well, better, or more efficiently than most other agencies that you know of?
- Which of your capabilities and services provide the most value to your clients or are most unique or particularly innovative?
- What are you truly passionate about?
- If you could only provide one service, what would that be? What services would you give up to have that focus?

For example, inbound PR and the ability to use data and measure results could become your area of expertise because you would choose to focus on it.

Bear in mind that specialization or differentiation around core competencies doesn't have to be based around a particular industry or vertical (health care, education, B2B, B2C, for example). It could be based around:

- A specific consumer audience or market segment such as millennials, women, seniors, Latinos
- Company size (small and medium enterprises, enterprise, blue chip)
- Geographic location (European Union; DACH or Germany, Austria, and Switzerland; Latin America; London; and so on)
- Particular brand values such as sustainability or social missions

STEP 5: DEFINE YOUR HOW

The *how* part is about making decisions and the way you execute them. It's about the internal processes and methods that you have to grow and train your team as well as the way you find and service clients. It's about your agency's culture and the values and principles that guide each and every member of your team.

Think about:

- What are the formal and informal standards by which your agency makes decisions about serving its clients?
- What are the formal and informal standards by which your agency hires, educates, and promotes employees?
- What is the one thing that you would never change about your agency?
- Will you say no to a prospective client because of your values and culture? If so, what are some of the reasons that would cause you to say no?
- Regardless of their role, what does it take for members of your team to truly succeed at your agency?

A strong values-based, documented culture is important not only because it motivates and encourages your teammates to excel at what they do, but also because it helps them make decisions.

In addition, it's a great resource for recruitment because people will be fascinated with how different your culture is and they will want to be part of it.

STEP 6: CREATE YOUR POSITIONING STATEMENT

The goal of this step is to help you align the four key elements you already defined in order to develop a simple but a unique-to-you agency positioning message.

Here's how you can craft your positioning strategy statement—simply fill in the blanks you see in Figure 5.1.

It's important to take your time crafting this. But please don't focus on the fancy words. This needs to be clear and to make sense. It needs to be relevant to your agency and it needs to be memorable. This is the only way it can be used—by your team and by your clients or potential clients. So don't over-complicate it.

Also, this is not a mission statement nor a vision. This is a strategy statement. Mission and vision are based on beliefs, hopes, and aspirations. They're part of your WHY, but they're not strategy. The positioning statement is. Why? Because it can

Agency Positioning Strategy Statement

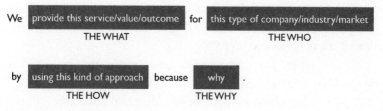

FIGURE 5.1 Positioning Strategy

guide all of your activities—your communications campaigns, your messaging on your website, which clients you approach, how your salespeople approach them, how your team delivers your services, and how you explain who you are and what you do at a networking event—in one sentence.

STEP 7: BRING YOUR POSITIONING TO LIFE

Now that you have your positioning statement ready, you can't just stop there after all that hard work. You need to make sure you align your team as well as your internal and your external activities with it.

The first step here is to sit down with your teammates and validate the positioning strategy. Does it make sense to everyone in the organization? Does everyone understand it? Would everyone use it in their day-to-day work, for example, by making sure that when approaching new clients they fit your buyer persona profile?

Next, you need to update the messaging on your website or any collateral you have. Can you put the positioning statement right on your homepage above the fold so that whenever people come to your website they understand right away what you do and who you do it for. If they don't fit the profile—whether as a client or even as a prospective employee—they will leave on their own and you won't waste any time chasing the wrong people.

Then, think about content campaigns you can start to promote your positioning. Can you create an e-book that is completely targeted at your best-fit clients and their biggest challenge, tying it to your unique core competencies? Once published, promote the e-book with a landing page, blog posts, social messages, and so forth.

In addition, you can create a team video that becomes a symbol of your positioning and shows how your people are part of it. What about going a step further and turning this into a media campaign as well?

Not doing this work is basically failing to market yourself. It's failing to create a sustainable agency machine, fully aligned internally and externally around why you exist, whom you service, what you offer, and how you deliver this.

Essentially, this is all about transforming your agency business model when you add inbound PR services into it. The best example here is PR 20/20 from Cleveland, Ohio, that started as a PR agency and has now become a performance-driven inbound marketing agency because it uses hybrid talent and advanced marketing technology such as HubSpot, Hootsuite, and Salesforce that enable a data and metrics mentality within its services and team capabilities. As an outsourced marketing team, PR 20/20 services the small- and medium-sized enterprises (SME) market, with inbound strategies they focus on enterprise companies. The company's story is quite interesting and I suggest you read about it on the company's website, at www.pr2020.com/story/history.

Remember, positioning is not a one-off. Things change. Markets change. Consumers and clients change. You and your positioning need to adapt with time as well. So do revisit this process in 3, 6, and 12 months' time.

How to Do Lead Nurturing and Fill Your Sales Funnel

The great thing about practicing what you preach and truly communicating your positioning is that you end up generating leads, and more importantly, not any leads but the right leads because you've created content specifically for your best client aligned with your positioning strategy.

On top of that, your sales team is also well aware of your best-fit client profile because positioning is a team sport and needs internal communication as well.

Knowing who your ideal client is, sales can now start looking for good fits among your leads.

Sometimes these leads are not ready yet, however. They haven't gone through enough steps of their decision-making journey. They need a bit more information—relevant information based on what they already know and the type of content they've consumed from you.

There's a very easy way to give them that—lead nurturing.

Lead nurturing is a series of e-mails specifically designed to bring a lead from one stage of the decision-making journey to another through helpful content in a timed sequence. (Some call this e-mail drip campaigns or marketing automation.)

Your buyer persona and the buyer's journey here are key because without defining them, you won't be able to develop a lead nurturing plan that actually works. You need to design the e-mails with the goal of answering the questions your buyer persona still has to get them to become an SQL—a sales-qualified lead that you can close.

Let's say that your buyer persona is Nick, the owner of an SMB (small- and medium-sized business), who understands that social media and communications is the future but he knows that he doesn't have the skills, the time, or the resources to do that. He's starting to learn more about what this whole new social media thing is, what the benefits are, and what the returns are, and eventually he comes to the conclusion that he needs to hire an agency (a partner) to help him with social media activities. Nevertheless, he's a little hesitant because this might be a big investment, and he wants to make sure that this long-term relationship is going to work and is not going to just cost him a lot of money or result in problems dealing with an agency.

In addition, there are so many agencies out there that he doesn't know where to start. Picking one seems hard. So he decides to check out the websites of the five agencies he's narrowed his choice down to.

He goes to each of their web pages, learns about their services, reads Team and About Us stories, specifically search-ing for something to show that these agencies know what they are talking about when it comes to social. He also looks at their social media profiles on Facebook, Twitter, and LinkedIn because he thinks that if they are offering social media as a service they better be using these platforms themselves.

Let's say you are one of the five agencies.

Since you've been active on social media, Nick finds a link on your Facebook page from your blog about the 10 pitfalls for SMBs when they create a social media strategy. The blog post covers exactly what he needs to learn more about. Luckily, you've also written a short white paper about creating a social media strategy for SMBs that works so this sounds perfect to him as he reaches the bottom of the blog post and sees the call-to-action (CTA) to get the white paper. He clicks on it and comes to your landing page, fills out the form on it, and off he goes to read the white paper.

On another agency's website, however, he finds an e-book on a similar topic so he now gets confused. What makes you stand out, however, are your actions after he's downloaded the white paper.

A day later, you send Nick a follow-up e-mail to ask whether he found the white paper helpful. He thought that was a nice touch but he's not ready to answer and talk to you yet. The other agency has reached out to him with a heavy sales approach right away and this has scared him. You, on the other hand, wait another three days and send him an e-mail offering him an e-book about getting started with social media for SMBs. The blog post he read from you was about the mistakes he should avoid when creating a social media strategy, the white paper gave him practical tips on how to do it, and now this e-book is providing actionable advice on implementing that strategy. This completes the circle and now he has an array of knowledge about his problem thanks to you.

Because he's downloaded the e-book, two days later you send him an e-mail with a blog post about why SMBs should partner with an agency for social media help. He certainly felt overwhelmed with everything that was listed in the e-book as a must-do so he clicks to read it. As soon as he does, you'll send an automated e-mail to notify your sales team so they shoot Nick a quick e-mail to ask if he wants to discuss how the agency could potentially help him. He responds: "Yes, let's talk." He now feels safe and his pain is even more acute and urgent because you've helped him understand it better.

You got him to be ready for a conversation with your targeted content that covers his buyer's journey, educating him more about his problem, and convincing him that to fix it he needs help. Your vehicle was the e-mails that you designed to nurture him. What's even better, you've fully practiced what you preach and he has now experienced himself what you can do for his customers.

One mistake that I see being made often is to want to do lead nurturing without the content to support it. As you saw in this example, without the appropriate decision-journey stage articles, e-books, white papers, videos, or blog posts, you cannot design e-mails that are going to be helpful and targeted.

You need to have everything ready for the next step to implement such a lead nurturing strategy, and you need to know your buyer personas really well.

It's the same when you do lead nurturing for your media personas—you need to be aware of the next step they'll make and already have the solution for it.

But why bother to go through so much planning? Because nurtured leads experience a 23 percent shorter sales cycle.[6] In addition, companies that use lead nurturing to move prospects further down the funnel experience a 451 percent increase in qualified leads and these leads make 47 percent larger purchases than nonnurtured leads.[7]

You are basically using your website and your content to sell for you 24 hours a day, every day.

Ultimately, it's also about you making a choice whether to work with this potential client or not.

If you design a campaign that covers the pain points of your buyer persona throughout the decision-making journey, you are basically testing them, as they are testing you, to see if they are a good fit for you. If they click on your e-mails and read your e-books, it means that they are genuinely interested. They want to learn. They want to grow. That's what you do because your goal is to enable that growth.

With lead nurturing you design click-to-close experiences. The better the experience is, the shorter the sales cycle becomes and so the lower your cost to acquire a new customer becomes.

Chapter 6

Delivering Inbound PR to Clients

Defining Inbound PR Services

Now that you know how you can generate new business with inbound PR, it's important to map out your service offerings. You shouldn't be selling something that you can't deliver.

In Chapter 3, we extensively covered what inbound PR is, so the process of adding it to your existing portfolio of services shouldn't be that difficult.

The easiest way to start is by making an audit of what you already offer.

Simply make a list of all of the services that you have right now. Often, with more traditional PR agencies the list will include media relations and event management.

To take this a step further, map out where these services fit with the stages of the inbound PR methodology: attract, convert, close, and delight.

This is going to enable you to identify the gaps of what you are still missing and what you potentially want to add. It also gives you a strategic structure that is easier to explain to clients because it has a starting point and an end with all the appropriate steps within each stage.

I also recommend thinking about where these services fit within the PESO model—paid, earned, shared, owned. This is going to allow you to discover additional offerings that could fit within the stages of the inbound PR methodology. An example here would be native advertising on Facebook as part of attract or even convert if we take Facebook lead ads.

What you'll probably discover here is that you have some outbound PR activities that you'll want to flip into an inbound version.

When we talk about outbound and inbound, this is how you should think about it: outbound means pushing messages out there to journalists or potential customers so that they go out and hopefully reach as many people as possible; inbound means pulling the right people in with relevant messages that they find on their own and choose to consume of their own will whenever they decide to.

Let's take a look at some activities.

MEDIA RELATIONS

We've spent a whole chapter on how to do media relations the inbound way, but the main point is that in the digital world, there's no need for nonstop journalist cold calling and mass e-mailing to pitch your story. Don't chase journalists. Give them a reason to chase you or the business you represent.

Just as with customers, you can pull the media in with relevant content that they can find when they do research. You can do this by turning your (dry) press releases into more engaging, keyword-optimized blog posts, videos, or even infographics and additionally creating an inbound PR news-room on your website where you can store all of this, including your press releases, for future reference and a search bank for the journalists that poke around your website (see Chapter 4).

And then of course, you can still do your media outreach, but do it in a way that the journalists you want to target prefer, meaning that you need to do your research about them, too, and be on point on the right channel, whether Twitter or LinkedIn or with a comment on an article they've written. You're moving to digital or social media outreach as a service.

RESEARCH AND REPORTS

This is another type of content that PR people usually take care of—the presentation of big research and reports (for example, yearly reports, sustainability reports, and so on) and then sharing them with the media.

What I find most shocking is that so many of those highly valuable PDF files filled with lots of information are just put on the website as a free downloadable link, and anyone can get a free copy of a report that's taken months or a whole year to create. And you can't even measure how they end up performing.

Here's a solution for you. Keep the PDFs, but instead of offering them as a free hyperlink, create a landing page where you ask people to fill out a form with their name, e-mail address, company (or whatever information you need) and only those who fill it out can get the report. By doing this, you don't give away valuable pieces of content for free, but you exchange them for contact details that you can use to engage with these people further as they've clearly shown interest (they filled out that form, right?).

This is how you add lead generation to your services.

Guest Posts

Speaking of all the content just mentioned—press releases, infographics, research, and reports—don't stop at hoping to gain some earned media through inbound media relations.

Go a step further and offer to write guest posts on relevant online magazines or blogs for your clients. You'd be surprised how appreciated such pieces of work are (provided they are relevant and of interest to the publication's readers).

This will allow you to share your client's content in their own words (written and controlled by you), achieve more reach and audience attention, and most importantly, get some link building going because usually the publication will reference you as the writer and link to the website and social channels you agree on. Having a number of authoritative websites linking to your client's website is extremely important for SEO and getting their page higher in search results.

This way, you not only add guest writing but also SEO as a service offering.

BROCHURES AND CATALOGUES

Another thing I've seen PR people do a lot is creating collateral. Brochures, catalogues, all those print materials being transmitted here and there. Don't get me wrong, such materials are needed at events, for example, but why leave it there? Why not turn them into infographics, PDFs hidden on landing pages in your inbound PR newsroom, or even better, mobile apps for people to browse and learn more or quizzes and bots to find what's best suited for their needs?

Interactive content is growing in importance so now is the time to repurpose all those materials and collateral your client already has for the online world.

This allows you to integrate content audits and repurposing into your services.

The world we live in today is a constant fight for attention because of a complete saturation of content; information is everywhere, all the time, from anyone, brands and ordinary people alike.

To build a sphere of influence in such a tough environment is a hard job. That's what you are promising your clients.

To stay relevant and manage to break through that attention bubble, you need to find ways to be where your client's customers are and that means stepping out of your comfort zone and embracing all the possibilities that digital offers.

Having done an audit of your existing services and considered how you could turn them from an outbound version to an inbound option or what other offerings you could add, now it's time to categorize them.

Often this exercise will allow you to create an inbound retainer—a repeat package of services that you deliver monthly for a certain amount of time, usually a year.

FULL INBOUND PR RETAINER

A full spectrum of inbound PR services could include:

Attract Inbound PR Services

◆ Persona development
◆ Content strategy (decision-making journey)
◆ Content plan
◆ Blogging and guest writing
◆ Press releases
◆ Interactive content (infographics, videos, bots, or apps)
◆ Keyword research
◆ On-page SEO
◆ Social media publishing
◆ Social media management
◆ Pay-per-click (PPC)

Convert Inbound PR Services

◆ Content creation (e-books, videos, infographics, and so on)
◆ Lead generation with landing pages and CTAs
◆ Inbound PR newsroom, build and manage
◆ Media database management
◆ Retargeting
◆ Content audit and repurposing

Close Inbound PR Services

◆ E-mail marketing
◆ Lead nurturing
◆ Thought leadership
◆ Social and digital media outreach
◆ Events
◆ Exclusives and interviews

Delight Inbound PR Services
♦ Social media management
♦ Research and surveys
♦ Link building
♦ Community management

Ongoing Inbound PR Services
♦ Weekly check-ins and performance reporting
♦ Campaign performance reporting
♦ Crisis communication
♦ Monthly strategy/review meetings
♦ Monthly measurement
♦ Quarterly ROI reporting

Once you have a list of the overall services that you want to provide, you should ideally break each service into all the small parts that it includes. For example, persona development is made of research, client meetings, customer surveys and interviews, analysis of data, and putting together the persona document or one-pager for distribution to the client and their marketing and sales teams.

By doing so, you will ensure that you don't forget key pieces of work that need to be done and also that you need to charge for. Often, agencies end up over-delivering and being underpaid for activities they perform but simply forget to add in their service packages and pricing. This happens when they don't have visibility into all the things that they are doing for their clients because they forget to monitor and track the time it takes for each deliverable. If you break your services down into its smallest parts, you and your team will know what to track and will be able to identify exactly where to stop and say no.

In addition, such a detailed list of services will enable you to package your offerings better.

Packaging Inbound PR Services

Now that you have an idea of what you should or could be offering, let's take a look at how you could be packaging it.

Generally, clients are skeptical when a new service is introduced to them or when they are asked to start a long-term engagement, say a 6- or a 12-month agreement. This is called a retainer; it has a monthly fee to be paid for the length of the engagement and includes particular services you are going to do for the client as agreed during the sales process.

Retainers are fantastic because they represent sustainable revenue that's always coming in and for which you can plan.

With the inbound PR methodology, it's really easy to develop a retainer offering. The stages of the methodology allow you to map out a full year of services that you can deliver with a particular focus for each and a staggered approach to delivering more once you work through attract, then convert, then close, and then delight (and again).

Retainers are not easy to get signed, however, especially if you are trying to sell clients a new service you have just developed. They can also be tricky, if, say, the client-agency relationship goes sour three months into a yearly retainer.

To avoid this, I always recommend developing a different set of service offerings that starts with two test phases and then ends with a full monthly retainer.

PHASE 1: WORKSHOPS

After a few conversations, you and the potential client have seen that you are both interested in working together. To start the relationship, you can offer them paid workshops, for example a strategy or a persona development workshop where you all come together in a room to discuss the given topic. This is a fantastic opportunity for you to show your expertise while leading the workshop and guide the client to getting the most out of the day. It's also a great opportunity for both parties to meet different people from the teams and test the dynamic of work. You both are trying to decide whether working together month by month for 12 months would actually be productive, collaborative, and enjoyable. Twelve months is a long time to be spending with someone so the engagement better have some chemistry from the beginning.

PHASE 2: CAMPAIGN

Toward the end of your workshops, you should have defined some sort of a plan of action, for example, now that we have created a first draft of our personas, maybe it's time to develop a full paid campaign for a particular persona. This would include a lot of the attract and convert offerings such as content strategy and creation, blogging, press releases, landing pages, social media, and a little bit of e-mail. A campaign like this could be one to three months long. Within such a period both parties will continue to work together on a regular basis to get to know each other. The goal is to achieve results with the efforts that you are promising and to see if the client will keep his word as well. The latter is especially important when the client is required to deliver content to you. If the client doesn't respect deadlines, then it's your work and ultimately the client's results that suffer.

PHASE 3: RETAINER

Provided that the campaign has gone well and both parties feel that this can be a fruitful engagement, now it's time to put your retainer proposal together. At a minimum, this should include: goals of the client, what you are going to deliver, responsibilities and deadlines, as well as people involved from both parties and monthly cost. When the client signs, this is when you can go into your ongoing retainer delivery with weekly check-ins and monthly performance calls and ideally an account manager to be the main point of contact for this client and the rest of your team members who are involved in the implementation of the different services.

Phasing this in is comparable to the development of a romantic relationship. You are basically asking potential clients to "Like us, then love us, then live with us."

When you phase in a new client engagement this way you ensure that both parties fully understand what it would be like to get into a 12-month client-agency relationship and have already found a way to work together. It's a much easier setup into a retainer agreement that will prove successful for both parties.

And if at any stage during the first two phases something isn't going well, then you are not bound by a long legal agreement that you have to stick with. You can walk out. You've gotten paid for your workshops and/or campaign, the client has received strategy plans, content, and campaigns, and more, and now they have what they need to either continue on their own or find another agency.

This gives you the power to say no because you'd find out early enough that your team would not enjoy working with this client and that the relationship would be doomed for failure from the beginning. You have space to find better-fitting clients and focus your energy on positive relationships.

What you want to avoid by going into retainers is to work on a project basis. Projects that last for a month or a few months are never a sustainable way for you to have money in the bank because you never know what's going to happen next month or what to do if your biggest client cancels. You can't plan and when you can't plan you can't grow.

With retainers, on the other hand, you have a long-term outlook and know what's coming in. This allows you to build a scalable business model with the time and the resources to expand and develop even more capabilities to delight your clients and create true talent within your internal team.

Developing Inbound PR Capabilities

The skills needed today in PR are way beyond just writing and communication skills. Brands no longer care just about awareness and reputation.

PR people need to understand broader business, marketing, and sales-related topics, and make data-driven decisions. This is far more analytical and strategic than simple press release writing and pitching.

But, according to The Holmes Report, talent remains PR's biggest challenge.[1]

The PR industry itself has been notorious for not keeping up with technological development as quickly as its colleagues from, say, advertising.

The reason for this has been the lack of digital adoption into daily work. In the same research from The Holmes Report, digital is issue number three and has increased since last year. There's a major concern that PR firms are not mastering digital and other new technologies, as cited by a fifth of all respondents.[2]

Part of the issue is sourcing great talent, the other part is retaining and training people for the new reality, especially because digital is the biggest driver of growth, as The Holmes Report explains.

If you want to adopt inbound PR, you'll have to retrain your entire team because if you have even one person who does not buy into it, your whole organization will shutter.

With inbound PR, there's a need to understand typical marketing terms like "lead generation," "filling up a funnel from top of the funnel," "middle of the funnel to bottom of the funnel," and "lead nurturing." Why? Because this is how clients think. They want to know the numbers and they want to see how PR activities impact the bottom line. Measurement and evaluation are necessary skills. Your people need to be able to tie in the numbers in every conversation, activity, and action.

If PR people fail to think with business metrics in mind, budgets will shrink. PR's value will be diminished.

KEY REQUIRED SKILLS

To stay up front you'll need to teach your people the ABCs of inbound PR (see the Appendix). You should also get them to:

- Take courses for Google Analytics, Keywords, and Ads to grasp website analytics, SEO, and paid media better.
- Complete the inbound Marketing and inbound Sales certifications from HubSpot, which are free, to learn more about setting goals, lead generation, and content for inbound.
- Learn the PESO model inside out and start thinking beyond media relations and press releases but develop new, more creative ideas.
- Master tools like Moz, SEMrush, Hootsuite, and Buffer to feel more comfortable with technology, automating activities, and measuring them. PRStack.co is the best resource to give you a list of free and paid tools.
- Truly understand the inbound PR methodology by having them run an inbound PR campaign for your agency.

Going a step further, you should look at how you deliver inbound PR services. It shouldn't be a list of things your people need to figure out when to do. You need to identify when they need those skills and how they build upon each other.

When you have new hires, develop a training program for them month by month for the first three months. This will be their onboarding process. Start backward: What do they need to know and be able to do by the end of month one? List this in its details. This will give you cues as to what you need to teach them so that you can figure out how best to provide training, whether it be through courses, training sessions, mentoring, one-on-one meetings, and so on. Then continue with the rest of the months. Most importantly, document this process to avoid wasting time and energy doing this again for your next hire. You can simply use this plan on an ongoing basis moving forward, and, if needed, just make small adjustments to it.

You can apply a similar approach with your current team. Give yourself a deadline of when inbound PR needs to be adopted and work from this as an end goal, going backward to create a logical learning journey.

Once you've developed your inbound PR services, take that list and add two additional columns next to it. For each service, list the knowledge and the skills your people need to offer these services with confidence. Next to that, write down how you are going to enable them to succeed. Are you going to send them to do courses (online and onsite)? Are you going to bring in an expert to do that or are you going to run your own training program? Are there resources, books, certifications your people might use?

In addition, assess the current skills of each and every one of your people. You might be surprised that one of them has the knowledge on a particular topic to train the rest so you won't need to bring in external training.

This allows you to identify the gaps between what you currently have and what you need.

Build learning into your agency culture. Allow your people to share learnings from clients and projects they are involved with in a regular weekly or monthly meeting.

Go a step further than what happens in your agency and explore the broader marketing world and trends by running a monthly meeting that covers all the news around social, marketing, communications, SEO, and so on so that everyone is able to keep up-to-date. Have one person prepare for this and present to the group. The next time it should be someone else and so on.

Knowledge sharing is essential if you want to deliver remarkable client results.

At the end of the day, it's your knowledge and skills that clients buy because they don't have them.

You need to train your people and you need to create an environment where you enable them to learn and share knowledge with each other.

You need to challenge your team and create a culture where they can grow and develop a career by staying at the front of new technological and societal development. Otherwise, they'll find someone else who can give them such an environment.

Don't leave your people to figure everything out on their own. Guide them and then let them learn, be involved, and be challenged.

Delivering Inbound PR Services

Now that you have your retainers developed, you need to know how you are going to deliver these services. This ties back to your training as well so that you know that your people can do the work.

The best way to figure out your delivery processes is to map your client's life cycle.

I recommend doing three-month sprints, as I call them, and narrowing in on the specifics of each month.

But before you go into what the signed agreement looks like, don't forget that you deliver services before your official retainer begins, too—in the form of a strategy or a plan that you pitch to implement for the full client engagement. And if you are doing paid workshops and campaigns beforehand, you need to map these out, too.

The easiest way to do it is to list all the little things that they include: who is responsible for them and how long it takes not just to implement them but to prepare for them and to follow up after the implementation is completed. For example, who goes to the meetings with the clients, who prepares the presentation pitch, what resources do you need for it and who is involved in the creation, who does the design if any, what about actual research to prepare your strategy proposal, are there any other touch points with the client during this process, and so on.

Once you have this first list, then you need to write down and track how long each of these activities take you based on the people involved in them. I'm not a big fan of charging per hour but for any agency it's a must to know how long particular activities take you because otherwise you'll overdeliver but stay underpaid. If you can't cost your internal resources correctly, then you are hurting your margins.

Now that you have nailed your preretainer work, let's take a look at months one to three, making the assumption that you've signed a 12-month retainer agreement.

Mapping Out Your Client's Life Cycle

The beginning is usually the most intense time with a new client as you are just starting the engagement, and there's a lot to learn about them and to do to get them started.

You'll also probably have multiple people from the team involved—ideally one account manager or project manager to be the client's main point of contact and work with the rest of your people on various tasks; probably a writer, and if you do any design or web development then these specialists, too, and so on.

Here's where the fun begins. Write down each small task you do during month one, how long it takes you, and who is part of it. For example, the kickoff strategy and goals meeting includes the client, the agency's CEO, and the agency's account manager for this client—it takes four hours to prepare, three hours to run, one hour to follow up. Preparation and follow-up always get forgotten but if you consider them among all activities, they add up hugely in terms of time and internal resources. Continue then with the rest of your activities that you initially do such as campaign and content planning, keywords and media research, press release writing if a story is already there, and so forth, and put these in your time tracking software (if you don't have such a program, get one as soon as possible because without one you are not going to be able to track how long it takes to complete certain inbound PR activities which, in turn, will hurt your ability to plan your next client engagements and your pricing).

Do the same with months two and three, during which you would usually finalize all content planning, strategies, persona development, and finalization, and you will create the first inbound PR campaign.

After the initial setup is done, months four to six focus on getting into a normal routine with regular account management meetings and campaign activities. Depending on the client and whether they have fully outsourced to you, these would be weekly, biweekly, or monthly meetings or calls. Each call needs to have a goal and an agenda that allows your account managers to effectively run it. For example, the first call of the month could focus on setting objectives for the month based on the yearly priorities and agreeing on the tactics you would need to implement to achieve the objectives. The second call could be about generating ideas and brainstorming new things you could try, for example, Snapchat. The third call should be about checking on the progress of the objectives that were set up in call one and if there's anything needed to do more to hit them. The last call should focus on the performance review and analysis of the entire month that would allow you to see what has worked well and what hasn't, both in terms of the campaigns and also in terms of the ongoing relationship with the client. Reviewing the first inbound PR campaign at this stage will allow you to make some informed data decisions about the next campaign to improve results even more and will guide your regular calls, too.

Months seven to nine are all about learning from the past months and the results achieved, what needs to be optimized and improved, particularly by reviewing the initial goals that were agreed on in the beginning. Toward the end of month nine you need to start thinking about the renewal of your retainer that's upcoming in three months. You need to be looking at the value that you have been providing and how you can provide even more so that the client will choose to stay with you after the 12 months are over.

As soon as month 10 hits, you need to start preparing for a renewal conversation with the right decision maker at the client and do everything in your power to ensure that the next three months are highly successful.

Ideally, you'll have monthly reporting meetings or calls to share success and results on the tactical level such as placements secured, traffic increased, leads generated, social media campaigns run, and so on. These should happen between the people heavily involved in the actual work such as account managers at your agency and your main point of contact at the client.

However, this success reporting is not enough, so every quarter you should be having more strategic reporting conversations with the C-level people at the client where you should go over the high-level goals that impact the bottom line and how what you've done so far has affected them. This is where your expertise in measurement needs to shine.

It's also where you can discuss things like upsells of services and increasing your retainer because you are sitting in front of the right decision maker with the signing power. During these meetings, you are not supposed to be talking about the next newspaper article you are planning but about how collectively your agency has significantly increased the client's revenue, how their investment has totally been worth it and can be seen through the value that you have brought.

Mapping out your client's life cycle month by month and your involvement in it will help you create a process for your retainers, projects, or any client touch points.

By documenting this, you allow your employees to be autonomous because they know what needs to be done, at what stage, and by when. Also, when you hire new people, especially account managers, they'll be able to easily jump into this process because they have very clear written guidance and expectations of the work they should be doing with clients.

You can use simple tools such as Google Docs to write down your delivery process and playbooks or you can use your project management tool to create templates of tasks for different processes or stages, for example, months one to three as onboarding. I'm a big fan of teamwork projects and Realtime Board for this.

Finally, ensure that you track time religiously. You do want to know how long your employees are taking for particular activities because if you don't, you'll simply be hurting your own bottom line. The ideal scenario is to test these services on your own first, and track the time so that you can be accurate when pricing these for clients.

Delivering inbound PR services is all about constant learning. If you want to delight your clients, you'll need to achieve superior results, build professional but friendly client relationships, and really prove your expertise—that will make clients come back for more.

Conclusions and Key Success Factors

Inbound PR is a mindset change. It requires commitment and willingness to invest the time and effort, to dig into why it's different, truly accept it, and apply it throughout your entire organization.

Inbound PR is about being a change agent that's always improving and moving.

To excel at inbound PR as a PR agency, there are seven key success factors I strongly recommend reviewing now and taking a look at in six months once you've adopted some of the advice I've given you in this book.

The success factors include the following.

1. Clear Vision and Unique Positioning

The agencies that succeed at inbound PR are those that first and foremost undergo a complete transformation of their business model. This is the biggest hurdle because it's about making the conscious decision about where you want to be three years from now and what you want to be known for. It's often choosing to go digital and ditching the old traditional world of outbound tactics. It also includes deciding to focus on a particular industry or core competency that you want to excel at and truly learn to specialize in.

Having a clear direction and being 100 percent focused is key because if you don't know where you are going, how are you going to get there (or anywhere), how are your people going to help you get there? Your positioning is crucial both externally and internally; existing and potential clients will know what you do and what you stand for, employees will know your values and align their work with your mission.

The longer you wait to make the decision about where you want to go, the further away you're going to be from becoming a sustainable, profitable, scalable, and known agency.

2. Being Your Own Best Client

I can't say this enough: whatever services you offer—content creation, PR, social media, and so on—you need to be delivering them to your own business, always. You need to nail content and you need to nail the numbers. You need to prove to yourself that inbound PR works. Why? Because, first, you need to learn the methodology; second, you don't want to experiment on your clients; and third, you want to be perceived as credible and trustworthy. How are you going to do that if you're offering services to your clients that you don't seem to be using to grow your own business?

Also, do you want be seen as an expert in your field, a thought leader? In the digital era, that happens with content, a lot of content. One of my previous agency clients at HubSpot, for example, has hundreds of videos on YouTube. They do webinars, they blog regularly, they do live video when they travel, they Snapchat, and more. Using these channels, they generate 100 percent of their new business through their own marketing and PR only, and they've managed to triple their revenue in a year. The best part? Their customers are some of the happiest HubSpot customers. Why? Because they trust the agency's expertise and knowledge in inbound, seeing how well it works for the agency itself.

3. Hiring the Right People (at the Right Time)

This one is hard but so crucial. If you want to build a scalable agency you need people not just with the right skills (because skills can be taught) but with the right attitude: the drive to learn and grow, the willingness to be involved in your agency's future, and the desire to challenge you how to move forward.

Finding the people that are a good fit for your business and your clients is one thing, getting them at the right time is another. You need to be able to plan in advance and start your recruiting process as soon as you decide to transform your business. Because once you've made that step, the clients will come and you will need to be ready to service them well.

Getting clients through the door is the easy part, truly making them happy and driving results on an ongoing basis is the magic you need to build a scalable business. And you need people to do that. As an agency owner, you shouldn't be doing project management or service delivery, nor should your employees be working 24/7 to handle the workload.

4. Strong Agency Culture

Having a clearly defined agency culture has two key benefits: it helps with processes and it helps with hiring and training.

Your culture needs to be based on your core values that you need to make abundantly clear so that your people can recite them. These core values will guide everything they do and the way they deliver the work. They will guide how you teach and train your people, too.

Having defined your values will also determine your hiring standards; you'll be able to better decide whether the person you're evaluating will be the right fit for your team.

One important thing to remember here is that if you're going the inbound PR route, then you need 100 percent inbound PR buy-in, not only from your senior people but from everyone at your agency. Inbound PR needs to be embedded within your culture, processes, and standards.

5. Ability to Say "No"

As human beings, we have an innate desire to help. In the business world, that translates into the need for more profit and more clients. But one key step when undergoing your business transformation is the ability to say "no" to the wrong clients.

You don't want to be working with companies that don't have the budget or the willingness to grow or those that don't trust your expertise and want things done their way. These clients are not worth your time or effort, and as one of my previous agency clients used to say, "Let them be another agency's problem." The agencies that choose to say no early on are the ones set for success.

Another thing that agencies often forget is that being able to say no applies to your team, too. Sometimes you need to make the hard decision and let the wrong employees go. For example, if you have decided your agency will adopt inbound PR, the people who don't believe in it or don't get it have no place in your agency. They're only going to hold you back. Is that what you want?

6. TOP-NOTCH ONGOING CLIENT SERVICING

Sadly, agencies often forget that it's not just about creating that tremendous service offering plan that gets the client through the door; it's about delivering these services on an ongoing basis and driving real results. With inbound PR, it's all about the numbers. Having very, very clearly defined processes on servicing clients throughout the agreed engagement is crucial. What does the kickoff meeting look like? Have you set up key performance indicators with the client? Do you perform regular performance review calls with them, et cetera?

To retain clients, you need to delight them. Here's something you may not like. You need to spend more, not less, time with your clients. Build and document these processes for onboarding, retaining, and renewing and learn to be efficient at them and always optimize.

To succeed here you need to invest in your people, because it's their skills and capabilities that will deliver either remarkable or poor results. It's your internal knowledge, process, and culture that create external success.

7. Drive to Learn and Share the Knowledge

What lies at the heart of all we are talking about is the drive to learn and the motivation to grow by sharing knowledge internally with the team and externally with the world to be helpful and position yourself as an expert. You shouldn't be afraid of competition. Competition shouldn't be stopping you but motivating you even more. Inbound is a movement, but it still needs the bandwidth to spread, especially outside the United States, and this needs to happen collaboratively.

It doesn't just stop with gathering the knowledge; it's much more about sharing it with your employees, with your advocates, with your clients. One of my previous partners is well known for doing just that in the industry—they are educators, they teach and empower their clients to be experts on their own. That reputation alone brings them more clients.

This is what a successful agency is—a living, breathing, always growing, and continuously learning people-driven organization.

And inbound PR can be your wake-up call. It's an approach that's easy to understand and apply and is not a conventional way of thinking.

It involves a mindset change that will allow PR to reinvent itself and earn the coveted management seat at the table as a truly value-driving discipline.

Inbound PR is all about changing how we see and do things to stay fit for the future.

Appendix

The ABCs of Inbound PR

A: ATTRACT

Attract is the very first stage of the inbound PR methodology. Everything starts here—a consumer's journey, a client's discovery, a journalist's search, a blogger's experience. It's all based on how we make decisions today, which is fundamentally different than a few decades ago simply because technology has given us so much choice and power. With inbound PR, you need to have deep knowledge of all stakeholders in your or your client's business and define where and how their attract stage begins so that you can turn them from strangers into visitors and readers of your content, and ultimately into paying customers or media people you end up working with on a story.

B: BUYER PERSONA

The most central aspect of all inbound, whether inbound PR, inbound marketing, or inbound sales, is the buyer persona. Nothing works well without a clear definition of your buyer persona or, when we speak about media relations, of your media persona. The persona is a semifictional representation of your ideal customer or any other stakeholder; it's that deep dive into their problems and needs and the questions that your potential customers or good media contacts are asking before they make a decision to buy from you or work with you. You need to know this information backward and forward. If you don't, you won't be able to succeed at any of the steps of the inbound PR methodology nor will you be able to create relevant content.

C: CONTENT

Content is at the center of inbound PR. It's the one thing that PR people excel at far more than any other professionals out there. Content creation includes things like blog posts; press releases; special content offers like e-books, reports, or white papers; videos; and interactive storytelling. All these allow you to enhance your reputation and build your expertise. Here we come back to the attract part; people will come to you because you create relevant and engaging content, either for buyers or for the media and through the media. And this is all inbound. It's pulling people in with blogs, then converting them into leads with relevant content offers, and then closing them as customers with a targeted sales approach that is still supported by good content in personalized e-mail.

D: DELIGHT

Delight is the last stage of the inbound PR methodology and is the one that is almost always forgotten, although it really shouldn't be. It's also the one that PR can have a tremendous impact on because it's all about maintaining and enhancing relationships with existing publics, for example, customer engagement on social media or via e-mail with relevant content. The same goes for the media or bloggers you've already cooperated with; engage with them even further by sharing their work or commenting on it to spark more conversations. Why is this so important? Because acquiring new customers is generally a lot more expensive than retaining existing ones. Similarly, developing a relationship with a new influencer takes a lot longer than nurturing existing relationships and capitalizing on them. In addition, the delight stage includes activities such as surveys and research that allow you to further understand your stakeholders and their needs as well as to gather accurate data for better decision making with your client.

E: E-MAIL

A greatly ignored or poorly done tactic in communications is e-mail. That's a shame because e-mail has such big potential, especially when we are talking about PR combining forces with e-mail. In fact, e-mail is the most effective tactic for lead generation and it's not that hard to implement. Because PR people understand audiences so well and are great content creators, they are well suited to craft good e-mails. E-mail is not only a must in the close stage of the inbound PR methodology but also in delight because you can continue engaging with existing customers or the media with personalized e-mails and content that truly add value.

F: FACTS

Give me the facts—you hear that from journalists a lot and from customers, too, when they want benchmarks. And often what works really well for content offers is to create reports with the results of a study or research you have done for your client or your business and industry. Because we love data on such a deep level and we always need the latest, people will be interested to hear your facts. The media will, too. So use data and facts wisely in your content and throughout all paid, earned, shared, and owned channels.

G: GOOGLE

You'd better not ignore Google in your inbound PR efforts. It seems that SEO has escaped the attention of PR professionals, but with inbound PR you simply cannot leave it out. Because for attract to work, for you to be found, you have to understand how Google works and how it ranks content. Then you have to create a relevant keywords strategy based on what your buyer or media personas search for and then create the content. Finally, you must optimize the entire website with technical on-page SEO. None of the rest of inbound PR will work if you don't do this.

H: HISTORY

So many PR or marketing professionals start working with a new client or on a new campaign and approach everything completely anew, forgetting to do some research and analysis into the past first. The same thing happens when the client engagement or the campaign continues—three months in and no one looks into what has happened during that time but rather focuses on creating a brand-new content strategy and some fresh, new ideas. No, don't do that. Make your decisions based on past performance, look at the data to give you insights. Also, there's probably plenty of existing content that can be refreshed, repurposed, improved, or updated instead of you and your team spending time creating something from scratch. Define your efforts based on what's done in the past, what's worked, and what hasn't.

I: INCLUSION

People like to feel part of something; they like to be involved. So give them that; they'll be grateful and they'll reward you with some word of mouth. Include others in the conversation on social media or cocreate stories and content for your next campaigns with customers or other brands. People also want to hear from others like them so get your case studies going, create some videos with customers and include people in your storytelling. It's real life that matters when it comes to inbound.

J: JOURNALISTS

You can't ignore media relations even though PR is not only about media relations. Inbound PR focuses far more on all other channels, not simply earned. Still, earned plays a huge role but the way to achieve it has changed. Journalists now act just as any other customer; they do their own research online, they build their brands and have influential voices, and they have the ability to ignore you. You can use the inbound PR methodology to attract and engage them and to secure a media placement in a far more personal and customized way than just a cold e-mail or phone pitch. This is about media relations the inbound way.

K: KNOWLEDGE

You are going to have to know your industry or your client's industry very well. That's not only essential so that you can develop the buyer or media personas; it's important because you need to develop some business acumen to properly advise and achieve real ROI that affects the bottom line. Knowledge in this case also includes being able to do more than just write. PR professionals, I know you hate math, but sorry, you won't survive unless you acquire those broader business skills.

L: LISTENING

One thing I don't see PR people do enough is listening. Learn to listen more. Listen on social media, listen when reading blogs or newspapers, listen when you are at events, listen when in meetings. Listening helps you learn, it helps you get to know the audience, the client, the media. It's how you then make informed decisions and how you build relationships. Listen and show real interest. Then conduct outreach in a personalized manner or advise correctly. Listening is all about diagnosing before prescribing. Don't skip this step.

M: MEASUREMENT

Oh dear, measurement, PR's biggest challenge! Anyone who works in PR hears this multiple times a day. The issue with not being able to properly measure PR activities has been around since the birth of PR. But with inbound PR, that goes away. With digital in general, you should be able to measure any activity from all paid, earned, shared, and owned media and tie it back to your investment, time, and efforts. You just have to connect the dots and do everything according to the goals you've defined in the beginning and bring all measurement back to them.

N: NEWSROOM

Companies should start utilizing their websites better. Here, I'm not only talking about lead generation and blogging but also about creating an inbound PR newsroom that serves the media well. Not only have consumers changed, so have journalists and bloggers and YouTubers. The way they prepare a story is different. They now do their own extensive research online and on social media, just as consumers do. They will find your website and poke around. Even if you've pitched something and they haven't found you on their own, they will still check out your website. So why don't you make it easy for them to get the information they need? That's simple to do—get a newsroom on your website and put press releases, relevant downloads, interviews, and whatever materials your media persona would benefit from on it. They'll be grateful because you are saving them time. In addition, you will improve your SEO.

O: OFFER

Get creative with the offers that you put on landing pages to convert people or the media. We spoke about facts, research, and reports. Yes, those are great, but what else? How about some videos or webinars? Hidden live streaming? Some infographics or templates? There's so much storytelling you can do with formats other than text. People get bored when they are offered the same thing again and again. Attract and engage them in a better way; help them to not get bored.

P: PLANNING

You better know what you are doing. You can't achieve your goals without a solid plan. Planning is about choosing the right tactics, methods, timelines, responsibilities, and roles in order to achieve your goals. It basically means deciding how to get where you want to be. Consider all possible avenues and make a detailed plan that describes your daily, weekly, and monthly tactics and to-dos; which PESO channels you'll use; what content will need to be created or repurposed (and by whom) and then published and distributed, promoted, and worked on with the media. The biggest piece of advice with inbound PR is this: don't rush in before you know what you are doing. You can always adjust and adapt, and you should, but don't just do something for the sake of doing something.

Q: Quality

Yes, you need a lot of content to rank on Google, generate leads, or attract the media, but it's not just about the quantity. Your content needs to be relevant, meaningful, helpful, value-adding, and informative. This is more about quality than quantity, not only in terms of your communications, but also the relationships that you are building and the leads that you are generating. One quality lead with potential to turn into a customer or a media publisher is better than 10 who never will. It's the quality of your content and your conversations that matter, not the number.

R: ROI

The most favorite corporate buzzword: ROI! It goes back to measurement. So to repeat, PR has never really been able to tie its activities back to the bottom line. With inbound PR, that's possible. PR can and does drive sales. You just have to demonstrate it, which is possible with a methodology such as inbound PR and the help of some software. Getting there is more about changing your mindset and becoming comfortable with numbers and data.

S: Social Media

I think we are past the stage where every business doubted the need to be on social media. The issue that we are facing now, however, is that social media is not really done correctly or efficiently enough. Social media is essential for every stage of the inbound PR methodology. You need it to attract people to your content; you can use it to communicate with journalists and close a story deal; you should be leveraging it to continue delighting existing customers, clients, or bloggers you've worked with. You can only be successful at this if you commit the time. I mean a lot of time, not just ad hoc activities here and there. You need to be consistent and tie social media into the bigger picture.

T: TRANSPARENCY

Transparency is the fuel of influence. It's the fuel of trust. It's the fuel of relationships. It's the key to inbound relationships. It's the one thing that would ensure you don't end up in a situation where you'll need some serious crisis management. Transparency prompts companies to stop hiding behind the true agenda, admit shortcomings, be honest and fair and so appear human and authentic. This is very important because people want to do business with real people. You work in PR, meaning you build relationships with different publics—you can't do that if people don't trust you.

U: UNDERSTANDING

To succeed with inbound PR, you'll need to have a deep understanding of the inbound methodology in order to connect the dots. The same goes for the PESO model and how inbound PR fits with the different media types. I urge you to do as much learning as possible around all those concepts in order to see the bigger picture and only then to start applying the methodology to your business. Without this basic understanding of all fundamentals, you won't be able to leverage inbound PR to its full potential.

V: VALUE

Everything you do with inbound PR has to provide value. This is why it's called inbound—it draws people in because your content is useful, helpful, informative, fun, cool, creative, and innovative. It adds value to that person, that customer, that client, that blogger or that media representative. It's not about you, it's about them ("What's in it for me?"). Do everything with this thought in mind.

W: WORKFLOWS

Workflows are the mother of automation for PR people who have such busy schedules already. Stop doing things manually. Define the goals; establish the strategy; create the plan, the content, and the assets and then let the software do the work. It doesn't have to be HubSpot from the start (although it's great!); you can go with Google Analytics, Facebook Insights, Mail-Chimp, Hootsuite, or another tool. I suggest you take a look at PRStack.co to get you started with the tools to optimize your daily efforts and reduce manual work.

X: X-RAY

In our digitally driven world, nothing stays hidden—people can explode in rage on social media, they can freely express their opinions on their own blog or on Medium and LinkedIn. This is why, as PR advisers, we need to ensure that words are aligned with actions. It's this integrity that builds and guards a company's reputation as well as encourages people to come to us and trust us. Because they will put you under the radar; they will x-ray you. This is how we make decisions today: We go on Google when we have a problem; we search for it; we read peer blogs or social posts; we examine company websites, blogs, and social media presences; we compare and only then we make a decision. We don't even need to speak to a sales-person. We as consumers have the power, not businesses. You better ensure that your online presence can handle that x-ray.

Y: YOUTUBE

Video content is booming. Just think about how much effort Facebook is putting into it, and so is Twitter, Snapchat,

Instagram, and all the rest. But YouTube remains the second biggest search engine so SEO can be big here. And let's not forget all the YouTubers you should be engaging with for cooperations or campaigns. Leverage your own video materials but also make sure you are part of others' videos. Here's where some earned media would work wonders for you.

Z: ZEN

Zen is a Buddhist sect that practices meditation, which does not just help the individual self but ultimately benefits others. This is how inbound PR should be, too. It's not about you, it's about them: your clients, your or their customers, the media, bloggers, YouTubers, and each and every public you are involved with. All the content you create and the touch points you develop are for the benefit of each of those stakeholders. Otherwise, it won't attract, and if you don't attract, you cannot move to close, convert, or delight.

Notes

Chapter 1. Getting the Basics: PR and Inbound

1. https://moz.com/blog/consumer-survey-reveals-the-efficacy-of-inbound-vs-outbound
2. https://hbr.org/2014/10/the-value-of-keeping-the-right-customers
3. https://www.stateofinbound.com/
4. https://www.futureproofingcomms.co.uk/

Chapter 2. PR and Measurement

1. http://amecorg.com/2012/06/barcelona-declaration-of-measurement-principles/
2. https://amecorg.com/how-the-barcelona-principles-have-been-updated/
3. http://amecorg.com/amecframework/
4. https://amecorg.com/amecframework/framework/interactive-framework/
5. https://www.holmesreport.com/ranking-and-data/world-pr-report/research/growth-opportunities
6. https://www.holmesreport.com/ranking-and-data/global-communications-report
7. https://www.zerfass.de/ECM-WEBSITE/ECM-2016.html
8. https://www.cipr.co.uk/content/policy-resources/research/cipr-state-profession-2016
9. http://news.prca.org.uk/prca-digital-pr-and-communications-report-2016-launches
10. https://pracademy.co.uk/2015/03/02/measurement-remains-a-key-challenge-for-communicators-according-to-pr-academy-research/
11. https://www.mckinsey.com/business-functions/digital-mckinsey/our-insights/cracking-the-digital-code

Chapter 3. Inbound PR

1. https://www.briansolis.com/2011/09/end-of-business/
2. http://gazettereview.com/2016/05/the-highest-paid-youtubers/
3. https://www.facebook.com/blueprint/courses/journalists
4. https://www.shiftcomm.com/blog/press-releases-dont-work/
5. https://www.theguardian.com/media/greenslade/2014/apr/14/marketingandpr-usa
6. https://www.holmesreport.com/ranking-and-data/global-communications-report
7. http://releasd.com/5873
8. https://www.holmesreport.com/long-reads/article/davos-2016-5-themes-for-communicators
9. http://news.prca.org.uk/ave-white-paper-accepting-a-broke-system-is-surrender-of-the-worst-kind/
10. https://blog.hubspot.com/agency/competing-consultancies-agency-learn

Chapter 4. How to Do Inbound PR

1. https://www.youtube.com/watch?v=dnfwckhZiLc
2. http://mtomconsulting.com/lifespan-social-media-post/
3. https://www.ing.com/Newsroom/All-news/NW/-2014-Study-impact-of-Social-Media-on-News-more-crowdchecking-less-factchecking.htm
4. https://www.shiftcomm.com/blog/press-releases-dont-work/
5. https://www.iliyanastareva.com/blog/creative-pr-using-the-old-tools-a-chocolate-press-release
6. https://www.edelman.com/post/storytelling-age-social-news-consumption/
7. http://news.isebox.net/2016-journalist-survey/
8. https://www.redbullcontentpool.com/
9. http://news.lenovo.com/
10. http://news.isebox.net/2016-journalist-survey/
11. https://www.digitalistmag.com/lob/sales-marketing/thanks-social-media-average-attention-span-now-shorter-goldfish-01251966
12. https://www.howtofascinate.com/our-research/kelton-fascination-study
13. https://www.redbullstratos.com/
14. http://ioeassessment.cisco.com/learn
15. https://www.youtube.com/watch?v=-7q7j4nXgMw

16. https://www.youtube.com/playlist?list=PL_klSsc1II1ocHv9CHY-zyJNUPxdcGI6Y

17. https://www.youtube.com/watch?v=9X-_EEIhurg

18. https://www.youtube.com/watch?v=B2rFTbvwteo

19. https://moz.com/blog/consumer-survey-reveals-the-efficacy-of-inbound-vs-outbound

20. https://www.headstream.com/blog/the-power-of-brand-storytelling

21. http://digiday.com/publishers/guardian-robot-newspaper/

22. https://www.youtube.com/watch?v=OnXijAxiy8g

23. https://www.ted.com/talks/simon_sinek_how_great_leaders_inspire_action

24. https://www.thedrum.com/news/2015/06/22/infographic-80-people-want-brands-tell-stories

25. http://www.iliyanastareva.com/blog/how-to-become-a-break-through-storyteller-infographic

Chapter 5. Generating New Business with Inbound PR

1. https://www.quora.com/How-many-web-agencies-are-there-in-the-world-in-2014

2. https://www.b2bmarketing.net/en-gb/resources/news/research-news-businesses-more-likely-buy-thought-leaders

3. https://blog.hubspot.com/agency/niche-advantage-pr-agencies-specialize

4. https://www.ignitiongroup.com/propulsion-blog/going-where-no-agency-has-gone-before

5. https://www.youtube.com/watch?v=u4ZoJKF_VuA

6. http://customerexperiencematrix.blogspot.fi/2010/09/hard-data-to-justify-your-marketing.html

7. https://www.protocol80.com/blog/21-lead-nurturing-statistics-that-show-the-power-of-marketing-automation-and-workflows

Chapter 6. Delivering Inbound PR to Clients

1. https://www.holmesreport.com/ranking-and-data/world-pr-report/research/talent-challenges

2. https://blog.kissmetrics.com/lead-gen-strategy-results/

References

CIPR. 2017. "About PR." Accessed July 22, 2017. https://www.cipr.co.uk/content/about-us/about-pr.

Dietrich, Gini. 2015. "PR Pros Must Embrace the PESO Model." PESO Model Graph. Spin Sucks Blog, May 2015. http://spinsucks.com/communication/pr-pros-must-embrace-the-peso-model/.

Enns, Blair. 2014. *A Win Without Pitching Manifesto*. Nashville: RockBench Publishing Corp.

———— 2015. "Top Ten New Business Development Myths." Win Without Pitching Blog, May 2015. https://www.winwithoutpitching.com/top-ten-new-business-development-myths/.

———— 2016. "A Manifesto of Business Practices for Creative Firms." Win Without Pitching Blog, February 2016. http://www.winwithoutpitching.com/manifesto/read-it-online/a-manifesto-of-business-practices-for-creative-firms/.

Hogshead, Sally. 2010. *Fascinate: Your 7 Triggers to Persuasion and Captivation*. New York: Harper Collins.

HubSpot. 2017. "What Is Inbound Marketing?" (and Inbound Marketing Methodology Graph). Accessed July 22, 2017. https://www.hubspot.com/inbound-marketing.

Kawasaki, Guy. 1989. *The Macintosh Way*. Glenview, IL: Scott Foresman Trade.

Macnamara, Jim. 2015. "PR Metrics: How to Measure Public Relations and Communications." University of Technology Sydney. https://amecorg.com/wp-content/uploads/2011/10/PR-Metrics-Paper.pdf.

PRSA. 2017. "About Public Relations." Accessed July 22, 2017. http://apps.prsa.org/AboutPRSA/Publicrelationsdefined/.

Sarachman, Iwona. 2016. "It's Complicated . . . the Changing Relationship between PR and Marketing." *PR Week*, May 18, 2016. Accessed July 22, 2017. www.prweek.com/article/1395258/its-complicatedthe-changing-relationship-pr-marketing#EUoiLoJ8h0KwMi6b.99.

Solis, Brian and JESS3. 2017. "The Conversation Prism 5.0" graph. Accessed July 22, 2017. https://conversationprism.com/.

Watson, Tom. 2011. "Tom Watson Reviews the History of PR Measurement." The Measurement Standard: Blog Edition. Accessed July 22, 2017. http://kdpaine.blogs.com/themeasurementstandard/2011/09/tom-watson-on-the-evolution-of-public-relations-evaluation.html.

Watson, Tom. 2011a. "The Evaluation of Evaluation—the Accelerating March towards the Measurement of Public Relations Effectiveness." International History of Public Relations Conference 2011, 398–412. http://eprints.bournemouth.ac.uk/19076/.

Williams, Tim. 2010. *Positioning for Professionals: How Professional Knowledge Firms Can Differentiate Their Way to Success*. Hoboken, NJ: John Wiley & Sons.

Index